Educational Interpreting:
A Collection of Articles from *VIEWS*

CONTENTS

 ·RID PUBLICATIONS

© Copyright 2000 by the Registry of Interpreters for the Deaf, Inc. All rights reserved.

ISBN: 0-916883-31-0

No part of the material protected by this copyright notice may be reproduced or utilized in any form or by any means, electronic or mechanical, including photocopying, recording, or by any information storage or retrieval system, without written permission from the Registry of Interpreters for the Deaf, Inc.

RID Publications is a division of the Registry of Interpreters for the Deaf, Inc.

The articles published in this book are reprinted from the *VIEWS* newsletter. *VIEWS* (0277-7088) is published monthly, except for a combined August/September issue, by the Registry of Interpreters for the Deaf, Inc., 8630 Fenton Street, Suite 324, Silver Spring, MD 20910-3803. For information on how to receive the *VIEWS* monthly newsletter contact the RID Membership Department at (301) 608-0050 V/T, fax: (301) 608-0508, e-mail: membership@rid.org. Internet: http://www.rid.org. Fax-on-demand: 800-736-9280.

The articles contained in this publication do not necessarily represent the opinion of the Association.

Educational Interpreting at the Elementary Level

By Jennifer Mills
Educational Interpreter, Associate Member, Maryland

VIEWS, Vol. 13, Issue 3, March 1996, Page 1

The educational environment provides a complex array of challenges at any level. What is the role of the educational interpreter? Can it be defined in black and white terms? I allege the color is definitely gray, especially at the elementary level.

I often discuss the role of an interpreter with fellow professionals. It is interesting that our role many times is defined as what we are not rather than what we are. We are not an elementary school teacher; we are not a teacher's assistant; we are not a substitute; we are not a note taker; we are not a tutor; we do not have lunch, recess or bus duty. So what are we?

We are professionals. The way we interact with both faculty, staff, and occasionally parents as part of the educational team must always portray that fact. And, in my experience, we are teachers. We are language models for deaf elementary students, providing accurate signs and building sign vocabulary as students progress through the educational system. We also help foster independence in deaf elementary students. By asking them if they need interpreting services during specific activities or events, we enable students to experiment with alternative communication modes. This helps build self-confidence as well as prepare them for the real world.

Building a student's sign vocabulary is also an important part of any educational interpreter's role. This role must begin at the elementary school level. By using age-appropriate signs and introducing new signs on a regular basis, the interpreter enables students to increase vocabulary throughout their academic career. This sign base must also be reinforced by fingerspelling key terminology as well as names of individuals in the school setting. Fingerspelling needs to begin in kindergarten. The interpreter must allow students to create name signs once they become familiar with the names of teachers, classmates and staff members. A lot of fingerspelling might be hard on the interpreter's hands, but it allows the student to be part of the group all the time.

I previously worked for the Montgomery County Intermediate Unit in Pennsylvania as an elementary school interpreter. There, the entire Hearing Support Group tried to develop different ways of providing quality support services at all levels of education. One project I conducted, a weekly with the teacher of the upper elementary group was an "interpreter lesson." The objective of these sessions was to allow deaf students to experience an academic lesson using an interpreter. Many of the students only went out of the self-contained classroom for non-academic subjects and needed to prepare to go out for academic subjects. The teacher gave the lesson using her voice only, talking at a faster pace than she would normally sign to emulate other classroom situations. I came in and interpreted the lessons for the students. We tried to develop different skills in the students during these sessions.

First, the teacher and I moved around the room as the lesson was given to ensure the students understood it was their responsibility to be able to see the teacher and interpreter at all times. We reinforced that if they had difficulty seeing, it was their responsibility to either move or to raise their hand and inform the teacher.

Second, the teacher conducted question and answer sessions to ensure the students understood that they had to raise their hands and be called upon before answering a question - something they did not always have to do in their classroom of six students. This session also taught the students that the interpreter would voice everything. So if the student was signing "out loud" to a friend or calling out an answer, it would be voiced.

Third, the teacher conducted lessons where she introduced new vocabulary. I would sign and fingerspell the word as the teacher continued with the lesson, on purpose. This session taught the students that it was their responsibility to raise their hands and inform the interpreter if they were unsure of a signed or a fingerspelled word. This session also taught the students to ask the teacher if they did not understand what the lesson was about.

Fourth, the teacher and I would hand out different sentences using the same word but with different meanings (e.g., run, poor, fall, back). We would then ask the students to sign the sentences in ASL and discuss the various ways to sign the same word. This session taught the students to understand the meaning of what they read or said and then to choose the appropriate signs.

Fifth, the teacher and I discussed 'what if' situations with the students. For example: what if there is no interpreter present; what if you don't understand what the teacher is talking about; what if you don't understand what the interpreter is signing; what if you missed information because you were not paying attention; what if you have a question during a lesson? This session allowed the students to use their skills in real life situations and to discuss with their classmates, teacher and interpreter, different ways to solve situations that may arise at school.

Overall, the lessons allowed the students to experiment with various skills in a safe environment. It also allowed them to ask questions and gain the confidence needed to go into a classroom with an interpreter for an academic subject. By the end of the year, the students clearly understood their responsibilities, the interpreter's responsibilities and the teacher's responsibilities in a classroom situation. ■

Educational Interpreters on Child Development

By Brenda C. Seal, Ph. D., CSC,
Associate Professor, James Madison
University, Virginia

VIEWS, Vol. 13, Issue3,
March 1996, Page 14

Developmental Issues

Forty-two (42) educational interpreters attending a workshop on the cognitive, linguistic, and social development of deaf and hard-of-hearing students agreed to answer questions for which we have no absolute answers. These 42 interpreters represented a cross-section of educational interpreters. That is, their experiences as educational interpreters ranged from 1 month to 14 years, with 21% reporting having worked less than 2 years, 26% reporting having worked from from 3 to 5 years, 12% from 6 to 8 years, and 17% from 9 to 14 years experience (23% did not report their length of time as interpreters). Ten percent (10%) indicated they were working in primary settings, 14% in elementary settings, 10% in middle school settings, and 12% in secondary settings. Most interpreters (24%) reported working in combined settings (e.g., primary, middle, and high school) and 17% did not report their employment site. Their responses to some difficult questions are recorded in the chart to the right. ∎

Question 1: At what age or stage does a student come to realize that an interpreted message is that—interpreted?

Chronological Age	Number (percentage) of Responses
4-5 years old	12 of 35 (34%)
8-10 years old	17 of 35 (49%)
12-15 years old	2 of 35 (6%)
Varies from child to child	4 of 35 (11%)

Chronological Age	Number (percentage) of Responses
Preoperational	4 of 33 (12%)
Concrete Operational	24 of 33 (73%)
Formal Operational	1 of 33 (3%)
Varies from child to child	4 of 33 (12%)

Linguistic Stage	Number (percentage) of Responses
At single sign/word stage	3 of 35 (9%)
Sentence expansion stage	6 of 35 (17%)
When aware of different communication styles	22 of 35 (63%)
Varies from child to child	4 of 35 (11%)

Question 2: Is there a relationship between the onset of interpreting and a student's learning to be a consumer? (Are students who have interpreters in primary years better consumers than students who have their first interpreting experience at the 4th or 8th or 10th or 12th grade?)

Answers	Number (percentage) of Responses
Yes	18 of 30 (60%)
Don't know	9 of 30 (30%)
No	3 of 30 (10%)

Question 3: Does dependence on an interpreter during the primary years foster overdependence or independence during the elementary and middle school years?

Answers	Number (percentage) of Responses
Overdependence	1 of 35 (3%)
Independence	15 of 35 (43%)
Neither (depends on student, depends on interpreter)	19 of 35 (54%)

Question 4: Does a student benefit more from having a variety of interpreters or the same interpreter across the school years?

Grades	Variety	Same	Don't know
Primary Grades	11 of 35 (31%)	19 of 35 (54%)	5 of 35 (14%)
Elementary Grades	20 of 35 (57%)	11 of 35 (31%)	4 of 35 (11%)
Middle Grades	31 of 35 (89%)	1 of 35 (3%)	3 of 35 (9%)
Secondary Grades	31 of 34 (91%)	0 of 35 (0%)	3 of 34 (9%)

The Challenges of Educational Interpreting

By Doug Bowen-Bailey, CI and CT, Minnesota

VIEWS, Vol. 13, Issue 3, March 1996, Page 16

The 1995 MRID Convention and its associated workshops offered a great deal to educational interpreters in Minnesota. Beginning on Thursday, Bonnie Gonzales, Amy Hile, and Mike Cashman provided excellent examples of how ASL can be used for various academic subjects. On Friday, Laurie Swabey's presentation gave a variety of strategies for developing the component skills of interpreting from ASL to English. However, Gary Mowl's presentation on "The Semantics of Fingerspelling in ASL" spoke most clearly to me as an educational interpreter.

For some, this may seem ironic. I split my day between pre-school and kindergarten and for many interpreters, common wisdom dictates that fingerspelling should have limited presence in such settings. It is difficult for us, as adult professionals, to understand fingerspelling, so how can we expect young children to comprehend it? A point well taken...well, taken to task by Mr. Mowl. Becoming comfortable with fingerspelling is a question of exposure—which is why hearing interpreters who have limited experience seeing fingerspelling have such difficulty. But not using it with young deaf children serves to limit their language development and their perspective on the world.

Mr. Mowl presented an example from his own experience. On visiting the classroom of one of his own children at a school for the deaf, he saw pictures of Disney characters on the wall. The teacher pointed to one of Pluto and signed "dog," which astounded Mr. Mowl. "Who in the world," he later demanded of the teacher, "calls Pluto a dog? Everyone calls Pluto...Pluto!" "But these children aren't ready for fingerspelling," came the teacher's response.

Of course, the point is that Deaf children are ready for fingerspelling. Perhaps not ready to produce it themselves, but ready to be exposed to it, to grow comfortable with its presence as a part of ASL.

Gary Mowl's presentation did not limit itself to the importance of fingerspelling. On a deeper level, he stressed the responsibility of interpreters to model appropriate use of language which bolstered my belief that interpreters who work with young children must not only convey what is said, but how to say it. It is a big responsibility. There is certainly room to question the efficacy of having hearing interpreters serving as primary language models for deaf children. However, there is no question about the reality that it is occurring.

Unfortunately, the history of our profession is in direct denial of the reality that educational interpreters must also serve as language models. In the past two decades, K-12 settings have been, in general, training grounds for inexperienced interpreters who, as they develop their skills, "graduate" to higher-paying, more prestigious employment. In plain terms, they work with adults. Too often, the interpreters who work with young children are the interpreters most in need of models for their own language development.

And Mr. Mowl brings a question from the back of his mind: "Who is at fault for the poor performance of Deaf children in education?"

Minnesota is attempting to address this problem with legislation for Quality Assurance and accompanying funds for training interpreters. According to the law, "qualified" is defined as having completed an accredited Interpreter Training Program and holding national certifi- cation—either RID's CI and CT or NAD's Generalist Certificate (Level 3). Some educational interpreters have expressed that these measures do not really fit accurately with what they do. After all, our task is to work with children which requires a different set of skills than what is needed to work with Deaf adults. This is, in my opinion, a partial truth. More accurately, working with young children dosen't require different skills, but additional ones.

We certainly need to be familiar with the language of the children with whom we work; but being language models requires us to go beyond that, beginning with being comfortable with the language of Deaf adults. Gary Mowl, in explaining how he communicates with his own children, cautions us not to go to the level of children, but stay just above them, within reach, but always expanding their understanding of language, pushing the envelope of their comprehension. To do this, we must recognize the child's language, be comfortable with adult language, but most importantly, we must be familiar with the discourse that Deaf adults use with Deaf children. For though we ourselves may not be native signers, it should be our goal to provide that quality of language model.

None of this is simple to digest, nor in light of our societal values will it be easy to address. Working with young children is something that is historically compensated very poorly, despite our supposed national commitment to young people. So, the reality is that highly-skilled interpreters will continue to find employment in places outside of primary education. And other interpreters, in need of language models themselves, will continue to be a primary example of language usage for young deaf children in mainstream settings. This is a shortcoming of our profession, but far too often, a serious impediment for the education of deaf children.

Gary Mowl's question continues to haunt me: "Who is at fault for the poor performance of Deaf children in education?" There is no simple answer, but what is even more difficult is to move beyond assigning blame and begin finding remedies. I think that those of us who work as interpreters with young children must begin with ourselves. What can I do to be a better language model? How can I ensure that I am a facilitator, and not a limiter, of education? Quality Assurance legislation here in Minnesota requires us to ask these questions, but our commitment to the young children with whom we work demands us to find answers to them.

I wish everyone the best of luck. ■

The Professional Development Endorsement System for Educational Interpreters

A Module Curriculum for Educational Interpreters

National Interpreter Education Project
Northwestern Connecticut Community College

VIEWS, Vol. 13, Issue 3, March 1996, Page 34

Interpreting for deaf children mainstreamed into public schools requires specialized technical skills, a working knowledge of the fundamental principles and practices of the school, a familiarity with child and development theories, and an understanding of the differing roles of the interpreter in various settings.

Few interpreter education programs have prepared their students with the specialized skills needed for interpreting in educational settings. Many random workshops and courses have been offered on various related topics, but there has been no systematic approach to these offerings, nor any vehicle for the accumulation of credit toward professional credentialing.

In 1990, when Northwestern Connecticut Community College was awarded a national grant from the Rehabilitation Services Administration, they were charged with the task of providing technical assistance to programs and schools hiring and/or training persons to work as interpreters in educational and rehabilitation settings. Toward this end the Professional Development Endorsement System (PDES) has been developed to provide a framework for sequential education beyond the equivalent of a two year interpreter training program for this specialized setting.

Until the field progresses in its professionalism and ability to offer comprehensive, **specialized** baccalaureate degree programs in interpreting, the PDES will provide a credible system for the upgrading of interpreters' skills and knowledge. The present design of the system will also serve as a basis for more advanced courses and a full curriculum in educational interpreting.

Mission

The mission of the Professional Development Endorsement System is to provide a practical approach to the study of the theoretical foundations and technical systematic skills needed to interpret in educational and/or rehabilitation settings. It is designed as an interim continuing education system for those who have graduated from two year interpreter training programs, or equivalent, and are already employed as interpreters, but who have had little or no specialized course work in educational or rehabilitation interpreting.

Overview

The module system of the PDES provides an overview of developmental, educational, and rehabilitation processes so that interpreters can better understand their working environments in order to more effectively facilitate communication and provide other support services appropriate to their roles and backgrounds. More specifically it provides participants with the opportunity to:

• Examine and discuss the role, responsibilities, and ethics of educational interpreters in elementary, middle, and high school settings.

• Further develop interpreting and/or transliterating skills to meet the unique demands of the various levels of educational settings.

• Discuss and practice the concepts of effective interpersonal communication with and between peers, school personnel, students, administrators, parents, and community members.

• Become familiar with theories and practices in public education, education of deaf children, and child/language development.

• Develop techniques for communication and interpreting in the specialized areas of education for deaf students with disabilities and/or rehabilitation programs for deaf adults.

Prospective Participants

Prospective participants for the Professional Development Endorsement System will come from three groups:

• Graduates of A.A. level interpreter training programs.

• Interpreters who have not graduated from a program but who can demonstrate interpreting skills equivalent to the two year graduate.

• Special Students: working interpreters who may not be able to demonstrate equivalent interpreting skills. These students will be allowed to take non-skill related modules until they are able to meet the prerequisites for the skills related modules.

Endorsement Areas

Upon successful completion of a specified programs of study, participants can receive a professional development endorsement in three areas:
• Educational Interpreting — Sign Language, Oral, or Cued Speech

• Educational Interpreting for Deaf Students with Disabilities

• Interpreting in Rehabilitation Settings

The first two endorsement areas require completion of 15 modules plus an internship. The Rehabilitation Interpreting Endorsement requires 5 modules, including an internship. Internships in schools or agencies will provide supervised, practical learning experiences for participants. For those who are already employed as interpreters, the internships can be incorporated into their regular work schedule, or provide the opportunity to experience a different area or a different academic level.

An endorsement signifies that the recipient has undertaken intermediate to advanced level study, and is prepared to function in an entry level position as an interpreter or communication assistant in a public school or rehabilitation setting.

The Modules

The PDES contains modules that cover both theoretical foundations and skill development activities. The design of the system requires that a skills development module be offered concurrently with a theory module so that participants can build technical skills while studying important background information. The modules in Phase I of the system focus on skills development for classroom interpreting and important background information related to educational settings and child growth and development. Phase II modules provide practical, lab-oriented activities that will allow participants to further develop their skills and knowledge in educational interpreting.

Theory modules contain 15 hours of lecture and discussion activities, while several of the skills development modules consist of 30 hours of group and individual lab activities. Participants will have the opportunity for individualized practice through the use of videotaped lab assignments that can be done in situations specific to each individual.

Pre-and post-tests will be included in each module, allowing participants with previous course work or knowledge to meet the module requirement by examination. Modules of 15 contact hours in class are equivalent to one regular college credit or 1.5 CEUs, depending on the choice of the sponsoring college or agency.

There are several part-time formats in which the modules can be offered; weekend workshops, short-term courses, or week long intensive courses. Depending on the format chosen, estimated completion of the education related endorsements will take two academic years on a part-time basis; for the rehabilitation endorsement, one year.

For more information about this project contact: Albert T. Pimentel, Director, National Interpreter Education Project, Northwestern CT Community - Technical College, (860) 738-6382 ■

Educational Interpreters—My Experiences

By Marcie Harper, CSC, Georgia

VIEWS, Vol. 14, Issue 8, Aug./Sept. 1997, Page 5

As a holder of a Comprehensive Skills Certificate and Masters Degrees in Deaf Education and Drama, I am writing to tell you of my circumstances, to share ideas, and to encourage you in the practice of your profession in the organization (RID).

When my involvement with RID led me to Southeast Georgia eight years ago, I began my teaching career with a caseload of three students with hearing impairments— only one which was Deaf and required an interpreter. At that time, I was the only teacher for Deaf/Hard-of-Hearing (HOH) students. In 1989, Glynn County hired its first educational interpreter. Today, in 1997, our hearing-impaired program has 24 Deaf/HOH students, three teachers, and six educational interpreters. One teacher is in a self-contained class with five preschoolers, and the other teacher and I travel as itinerant resource teachers to two schools daily (splitting the middle and high school caseload). Because of our distribution this year, we have at least one interpreter at each of four schools: one preschool, one elementary, one middle school, and one high school.

A Special Pay Scale For Interpreters

In 1990, when our second interpreter was hired, we began to explore the possibility of a separate pay scale and an appropriate job title for interpreters. They were then classified as paraprofessionals (AKA teacher aides). We made contact with our state Department of Education Hearing-Impaired Consultant, Page Long, who was able to refer us to other counties that already had pay scales in place for interpreters. After

five years of advocacy with the Higher Powers by way of our Special Education Director, our Board of Education finally approved our recommendations. *Don't give up hope!*

Currently, our Educational Interpreters have a separate job description and a five level pay scale including:

(1) *Entry Level* (high end of paraprofessional pay);

(2) *Level 2* —100 contact hours in courses in sign language/deafness and an 80 percent rating on evaluation;

(3) *Level 3* — 200 contact hours of classes and an 80 percent rating or a degree from an Interpreter Training Program;

(4) *Level 4* — State Quality Assurance Screening Level; and

(5) *Level 5* — RID Certification: Same as beginning teacher pay.

Ideas For Building Self-Esteem and Reducing Isolation in Mainstreamed Students in Semi-Rural Areas

With a TV in each classroom, our schools use closed circuit televisions to present the morning announcements. It is the perfect venue for teaching mini-sign language lessons, spotlighting your student as a campus reporter, or promoting Deaf Awareness. Some schools have sign language clubs, choirs, or early bird sign language classes for students. We hope next year to offer ASL as an elective at the high schools.

At each grade level in elementary

and middle school, two teachers are targeted who are interested in working with Deaf students and are taking staff development sign language courses. Also, at the end of each year, the regular classroom teacher and interpreter identify a cadre of hearing peers with sign skills to place in the same class as the Deaf student during the fall of the next year. That way, the Deaf student has friends to communicate with comfortably.

Twice a year we have regional Deaf Field Days (in the fall at the park and in the spring at the beach), and we invite Deaf/ HOH students from neighboring counties to join us for a Day of Fun in the Sun. We encourage pen pal relationships with Deaf/HOH students nearby. Locally, students keep weekly journals with Deaf/HOH friends at other schools. Middle school students are sometimes paired with elementary or high school students, depending on their interests and writing skills.

For the past four years, our students have entered and been chosen by judges to participate in the International Creative Arts festival sponsored by the Center on Deafness in Chicago, Illinois. It's a wonderful weekend of fellowship, workshops, and displayed talent with about 300 students, parents, and professionals filling the pool, restaurant, and lobby with sign language! Students can enter a variety of categories including: performing arts, literature, art in any 2D medium, etc. For more information, write or call: Sandra Harvey, Center on Deafness, 3444 Dundee Road, Northbrook, IL 60062 (708) 559-0110.

We have a relatively small adult Deaf population and no active Deaf Club. Consequently, two years ago we started a Hearing-Impaired Parent Support Group whose primary goal is to provide monthly educational or social opportunities for our Deaf/HOH students and Deaf adults in the community. It also becomes a way to stay in touch with recent graduates from our program. We have silent suppers and covered dish suppers, go skating, bowl, camp-out, and cook-out.

Ideas For Building Self-Esteem and Reducing Isolation in Educational Interpreters

Since our interpreters and teachers are scattered to the winds, we all meet together once a month after school and quarterly on teacher work days to discuss concerns about our students, the program, and upcoming events (e.g., ASL workshops, interpreted theatrical events, standardized testing, field days, etc.). While the teachers are planning and preparing progress reports for the grading period, the interpreters get together to view video practice tapes, critique each other, and help each other with vocabulary, skill building, and ethical concerns.

Since most of our nearby hearing-impaired teachers teach in semi-rural counties and are often the only ones of their kind in their counties, we have in Southeast Georgia an active Consortium that plans bi-annual workshops to get hearing-impaired teachers and interpreters together to network and share ideas. These workshops are planned with the assistance of our regional Learning Resources Service Centers. For the past two years, at least one of the consortia has brought in interpreter trainers to focus on improving sign skills. Also, our state Department of Education offers in Atlanta an annual week-long Summer Institute for Educational Interpreters, and GRID has an annual Educational Interpreter Conference.

Conclusion

All of this is to say to my colleagues in the profession and RID, I know that you, too, have many insights, ideas, and activities that would inspire. Let us continue to encourage one another. ∎

Guidelines for Inservicing Teachers Who Teach with Educational Interpreters

By Brenda C. Seal, Ph.D., CSC, Virginia

VIEWS, Vol. 15, Issue 2, February 1998, Page 1

The growing number of deaf and hard-of-hearing students who have educational interpreters in their mainstream and inclusion placements offers new meaning to the terms "collaboration," "teaming," "partnership," "consultation," and "shared responsibility." Indeed, a common premise of any successful educational program is that the better the collaboration of those responsible for educating the students, the better the expectations for "educated" students. A common strategy in introducing and achieving collaborative programming in the field of communication disorders involves "inservicing" teachers. In these inservices, speech-language pathologists attempt to educate classroom teachers about their roles, the importance of collaborating with the teachers in fulfilling their roles and in maximizing the student's communication experiences (Achilles, Yates, & Freese, 1991; Magnota, 1991; Moore-Brown, 1991; Prelock, Miller, & Reed, 1995).

Sadly, the same push to enhance collaboration between speech-language pathologists and classroom teachers has not expanded to include educational interpreters. Less than 50% of teachers who have students with interpreters receive any formal inservicing on the interpreter's role (Hayes, 1991) or on the communication needs of their students (Flexer, Wray, & Ireland, 1989; Mertens, 1991; Strudthoff & Blair, 1996). Those teachers who do experience inservices report that they are most likely to learn about the types and severity of hearing loss, different amplification systems, the effects of hearing loss on academic performance, different communication methods and systems, and preferential seating (Strudthoff & Blair, 1996), and are

less likely to learn about the roles and responsibilities of the interpreter and the roles and responsibilities of the teacher who works with an interpreter (Beaver, Hayes, & Luetke-Stahlman, 1995).

One of the problems that educational interpreters may experience in attempting to collaborate with classroom teachers involves their own lack of confidence in designing and conducting an effective inservice. In fact, most of us have been on the receiving end of inservices that were too abstract or theoretical, lacking in credibility, poorly prepared and organized, not directed to the stated objectives, dated in the concepts being taught, and hurried with poor quality materials (Sommers & Caruso, 1995, p. 25). Additional complaints among educators who are required to attend inservices include a lack of teacher involvement in the planning of the inservice and failure of those conducting the inservice to provide a follow-up phase, either for evaluating what was to be implemented or for additional training (Brimm & Tollett, 1974). In spite of these common complaints, those few teachers who have experienced inservices about the roles and responsibilities of interpreters and how to work with educational interpreters reported them to be beneficial in increasing their understanding and expectations (Beaver, Hayes, & Luetke-Stahlman, 1995). The purpose of this paper is to borrow from these and other findings in providing guidelines for inservicing teachers who teach with educational interpreters.

Guideline 1: Consider your timing, terminology, and teachers

Inservices generally refer to in-house training or staff development on a particular topic or theme.

Preservice training generally refers to prior educational experiences that set the stage for or enable an inservice to be successful. Many general education teachers have had prior experiences in "special" education. These teachers may have taken a course in sign language or observed interpreters at their local churches. Their knowledge of deafness and educational interpreting services will no doubt be influenced by these experiences and "may prove to be a bonus or a hindrance, or may be altogether nonexistent" (Seal, 1998, p. 6). Determining the needs of the teachers, then, is important to successful planning.

Most school systems assign their inservice days according to an annual calendar. That is, some designated time during the first week of the school year is usually set aside; motivational inservices are likely to be held for large audiences and specific topic-centered inservices are scheduled for smaller groups. Teacher workdays during the middle of the year or at grading intervals may also be used to schedule inservices. Interpreters should determine from the administration if their inservice is to comprise a one-day-only event or if follow-up sessions will be scheduled. If we keep in mind the criticisms teachers offer about inservices, we can clearly see the need for follow-up. When follow-up inservices are NOT scheduled as part of the annual calendar, interpreters must find alternative ways to assess the impact of their inservice, preferably with written feedback and formal meetings at scheduled intervals. Closing the inservice with a written questionnaire and securing "three possible times at the end of this grading period to determine your answers to these questions" may be more practical and beneficial than "a second phase to this inservice topic next February."

Regardless of the number of inservice days allotted, interpreters should do a *needs assessment* as early as possible. Seasoned and returning interpreters can determine from their own experiences and from talking to or surveying teachers who taught with interpreters in the previous school year what issues, concerns, questions were most prevalent as they faced sharing their classroom, students, and communication style with a stranger. Newly hired interpreters should benefit from aligning with a colleague, either a returning speech-language pathologist or teacher of the deaf, who can shed light on the teachers' needs. Allen (1994) recommended preliminary planning for staff development to include "focus group interviews" (p. 494) with different constituencies: the "support staff" focus group, as an example, could include the speech therapists, counselors, interpreters, and teacher aides; the high school focus group could include the secondary teachers, parents, and interpreters. Questions to the focus group should be relatively consistent and focused on determining the most immediate and most common needs that should be addressed in the inservice. Conducting these focus group interviews at the close of the school year enables not only a good closure to that school year, but also enables planning for a good beginning inservice for the next school year.

Guideline 2: Determine who will present, what materials will be used, and what will be expected of the attending teachers

An inservice that focuses on the roles and responsibilities of the interpreter and the teacher might well begin with a silent period during which each participant lists what he or she "thinks" the interpreter's role should be and what he or she "thinks" the teacher's role should be when the teacher teaches with an interpreter. Guiding the participants with a series of questions posed on the overhead may establish a theme

of participation that will prevail throughout the inservice. Questions such as the following may also lead to a variety of responses that further leads to quality discussion during the inservice about the interpreter's and teacher's roles:

1. What should the interpreter do when the teacher is talking to an individual student at his/her desk?

2. What should the teacher do if the interpreter appears to be chatting with the deaf student?

3. What should the interpreter do if there's a substitute?

4. What should the teacher do when the deaf student doesn't pay attention?

5. What should the interpreter do during "down" time or when students are doing seat work?

6. What should the teacher do when the student talks to him/her and the teacher doesn't understand?

7. What signs, if any, should the interpreter "teach" the teacher? the whole class?

8. When should this sign instruction occur?

Another possibility for opening the inservice involves showing videotaped segments of teachers and interpreters from previous school years. The use of videotaped samples has been recommended for evaluations, orientations, and inservices (Schick & Williams, 1994; Seal, 1998). Short segments of personally collected tapes (with permission, of course) can be used to supplement or personalize commercial tapes (Madonna University and Sign Media's "Sign Language Interpreters in the Public Schools" (1992) tapes, Elizabeth Winston's "Interpreting in the Classroom: Providing Accessibility or Creating New Barriers" tape, as examples). Nothing is more UNsuccessful in an inservice, though, than a 45-

minute lecture on videotape, presented with lights out, in a warm room, following a large lunch.

Another possibility for opening the inservice involves a staged vignette in which a deaf "student" (perhaps a deaf teacher or member from the deaf community), a hearing "teacher" (perhaps a teacher who has taught with interpreters before), and an "interpreter" (perhaps a visiting interpreter) demonstrate a typical lesson. Questions can be given to the audience to guide their observations (e.g., What did the interpreter do when the student acted like he didn't understand? What did the teacher do when the student raised his hand to answer the question?) and serve as discussion topics later in the inservice. Rehearsing the role play is, of course, necessary to its success. A 5-minute role play may also be used later in the inservice to provide experiences for those attending and to open discussion for attitude questions (e.g., How did you feel when the student watched the interpreter instead of you? How did you feel when the interpreter waited until your second sentence before beginning to interpret? How did you feel when the interpreter interrupted you for a repetition?)

An additional possibility, especially for more didactic inservices, is to have the inservice presentation interpreted by a visiting interpreter. Inviting a deaf consumer to participate in the inservice, as a member of the audience and for the role plays or a panel or a lecture, etc., is also advisable to demonstrate the sign-to-voice role that interpreters must take when the student's turn to communicate occurs.

Each of these possibilities for opening the inservice—the silent period for questions and answers, the videotaped demonstrations, the role play, lectures with visiting interpreters and deaf consumers—suggests audience participation. Audience participation is always important to successful inservices, but, by the very nature of the inservice, restricts audience size to small groups. Of course, there is no perfect audience size, but certain common sense guidelines should be followed.

The larger the audience, the more valuable the topic is likely to be perceived. In contrast, the smaller the audience, especially if it's smaller than the presenting staff, the less prestigous the inservice will be perceived. An inservice that includes a presentation from the speech-language pathologist, the teacher of the deaf, a deaf student consumer (e.g., a high school student participating in an inservice for elementary teachers), and the interpreter should have at least as many participating teachers (perhaps the two third-grade teachers, the physical education teacher, the art teacher, the librarian, and the principal).

There is also no perfect inservice time allotment, but certain common sense guidelines should be followed. The longer the inservice, the more information can be shared (and remembered or forgotten). Short sessions, particularly if the inservice is well organized, may be more impressionable than longer inservices with too much to absorb.

Guideline 3: Determine how to close the inservice and how and when the follow-up will be scheduled

Planning the closing of the inservice is every bit as important as planning the opening. Like the closing argument of an effective attorney, the audience (the jury) is left to deliberate how much of the information (the testimonies) will sway a verdict of "valuable" or "a waste of my time." Presenters who are new to inservices are often guilty of over-preparing and rushing through the final 15 minutes of material in the last 2 minutes. Adjourning 5 minutes early is far more pardonable than running 5 minutes late. Careful monitoring of the time, then, is critical in coming to the closing. Setting aside time to summarize the major points of the inservice, to thank the invited guests and the audience for its participation, and to ask them to evaluate the inservice is important but often overlooked because of timing. A planned evaluation instrument, like a planned closing statement, and a planned follow-up, should be part of the inservice, not additions to it.

The evaluation instrument may be standard for the school system because of its generalities. When this is the case, an additional form on which the participants can list additional concerns, additional inservice needs, and possible follow-up meeting times enables more personal feedback to the interpreter without jeopardizing the anonymity of the evaluating audience members. Finally, the best planning for the next inservice begins with the evaluation of the current inservice. Discussing with those who presented what worked, what didn't work and why, is important feedback for the follow-ups.

Educational interpreters must be vigilant in their efforts to collaborate with teachers:

> Providing "clear, concise, and relevant information," minimizing jargon that others may not understand, and providing accurate information about the services being provided and the needs of the student are recommended by Hedge and Davis (1995, p. 142) as important practices in collaborating with other professionals. (as cited in Seal, 1998, p. 54)

A well-planned, conscientiously conducted inservice can set the stage for meaningful partnerships that mature over the months of the school year. "Being a member of a collaborative team empowers the interpreter to maximize her knowledge...in a way that maximizes the other members' knowledge...This membership is critical to the delivery of optimum services" (Seal, 1998, pp. 54-55).

References

Achilles, J., Yates, R. R., & Freese, J. M. (1991). Perspectives from the field: Collaborative consultation in the speech and language program of the Dallas Indepndent School District. *Language, Speech, and Hearing Services in Schools, 22,* 154-155.

Allen, B. M. (1994). A case study in planning staff development: What do teachers really need? *American Annals of the Deaf, 139,* 493-499.

Beaver, D. L., Hayes, P. L., & Luetke-Stahlman, B. (1995). In-service trends: General education teachers working with educational interpreters. *American Annals of the Deaf, 140,* 38-46.

Brimm, J., & Tollett, D. (1974). How do teachers feel about inservice education? *Educational Leadership, 31,* 21-25.

Flexer, C., Wray, D., & Ireland, J. (1989). Preferential seating is NOT enough: Issues in classroom management of hearing-impaired students. *Language, Speech, and Hearing Services in Schools, 20,* 11-21.

Hayes, P. L. (1991). Educational interpreting for deaf students: Their responsibilities, problems, and concerns. *Dissertation Abstracts International, 53,* 02a. (University Microfilms No. 9218857, 462)

Hedge, M. N., & Davis, D. (1995). *Clinical Methods and Practicum in Speech-Language Pathology, 2nd Ed.* San Diego, CA: Singular Publishing.

Madonna University (1986-1988). *Interpreters in the Public Schools (Videotapes),* Sign Media, Incorporated, Burtonsville, MD.

Magnotta, O. H. (1991). Looking beyond tradition. *Language, Speech, and Hearing Services in Schools, 22,* 150-151.

Mertens, D. (1991). Teachers working with interpreters: The deaf student's educational experience. *American Annals of the Deaf, 136,* 48-52.

Moore-Brown, B. J. (1991). Moving in the direction of change: Thoughts for administrators and speech-language pathologists. *Language, Speech, and Hearing Services in Schools, 22,* 148-149.

Prelock, P., Miller, B., & Reed, N. (1995). Clinical exchange: Collaborative partnerships in language in the classroom program.

Language, Speech, and Hearing Services in Schools, 26, 286-292.

Schick, B., & Williams, K. (1994). Evaluating educational interpreters using classroom performance. *Interpreter Views, 11,* 15-24.

Seal, B. C. (1998). *Best Practices in Educational Interpreting.* Boston, MA: Allyn & Bacon.

Sommers, R. K., & Caruso, A. J. (1995). Inservice training in speech-language pathology. *American Journal of Speech-Language Pathology, 4,* 22-28.

Strudthoff, J., & Blair, J. C. (1996). Providing information to teachers on educating students with hearing loss. American Speech-Language-Hearing Association Annual Convention, Seattle, Washington.

Winston, E. (199_). *Interpreting in the Classroom: Providing Accessibility or Creating New Barriers (Videotape).* Johnson County Community College, Overland Park, KS. ■

Improving Educational Access in California

By Lori Green and Virginia Northrop, Associate Members

VIEWS, Vol. 15, Issue 2, February 1998, Page 9

As Interpreters for the Deaf in a large northern California school district, we have encountered various professional difficulties and struggled with their resolution, just as many other educational interpreters all over the country. There are currently nine interpreters employed at 4 elementary, middle, and high school sites, serving a district comprised of 50,000 students, approximately 60 of whom are deaf.

The majority of our school district's interpreters are members of the local affiliate chapter of RID, and some have put in service to the local and regional boards. Most of us have prior or concurrent experience as freelance, community, corporate, and community college interpreters. It is that experience, knowledge, those ongoing relationships, and active participation in the developments in our field which has enabled us to work together as a cohesive group in furthering better service provision for the deaf students.

One of the reasons we have been able to entice such good interpreters to work for our district is a fair pay and benefits package. Our district does compensate state or RID certified interpreters at a higher rate of pay and it is also possible to earn additional pay increases through continued education.

We Interpreters for the Deaf have actively made great strides during the past 5 years, resulting in a slow evolution in the understanding of our profession and our role within the school district. We actively advocate that our district hire well qualified interpreters. In our push for quality, we sought a revision in our job description some time ago and it now includes a number of significant strengths, namely,

- Use of the mode of communication most readily understood by the hearing-impaired student.

- Participation, solely as a team member, during the student's IEP (if a deaf individual attends the meeting, interpreting is provided by a second interpreter).

- Interpreters are supervised by a Special Education administrator, not the teacher.

- Daily preparation period.

- Interpret for extracurricular activities and meetings or evaluations with other staff and professionals.

- Train students to become independent consumers of interpreting services.

We have never been classified as Interpreter/Aides. This is mentioned as a point of clarification, as that title is a fundamental stumbling block for many school districts, preventing dialogue about what a well-defined role for educational interpreters in K - 12 ought to be.

From the very beginning, certified interpreters from the community were brought in as consultants and were instrumental in developing the original job description for our position. Use of these consultants has been ongoing, as all prospective hires must take a performance evaluation. The school district and a consultant also worked with us in a cooperative effort to draw up an Interpreter Handbook. This handbook is extremely well written and something we can be proud of.

Despite all the advances in our working environment, difficulties persist. We constantly must educate and remind teachers and administrators we are working with about the necessity for interpretation and the nature of our role. Teachers and administrators are accustomed to making decisions without input from classified staff, and because they lack knowledge in the field of deafness, their decisions unknowingly result in exclusion or insensitivity toward deaf students. Working within this "educational culture" is problematic. The perceptions held by teachers and administrators generally relegates all classified employees to a low status, lacking in any authority or power. Classified personnel generally include classroom aides, school secretaries, custodial staff, food service workers, maintenance workers, and bus drivers. As classified employees we are represented by SEIU Local 22 (Service Employees International Union) which has been there at every turn, to assist and support our efforts as we strive to gain understandings. As a unique group of classified employees, gaining recognition and respect for our differences has been hard won.

Second, many parents of deaf children are unfamiliar with the role of an interpreter in their child's education. Because we work in a large, urban school district comprised of a very diverse ethnic mix, we often encounter students whose parents are themselves linguistically and culturally cut off from the educational bureaucracy, and who cannot advocate on behalf of their deaf children.

Some forward movement from forces outside our district gives us hope of improvement in these difficult areas. The Deaf Education Coalition, comprised of 26 member agencies and organizations representing deaf and hearing impaired people in California has entered into the dialogue. Their eventual recommendations will lead to better understandings about the unique needs of deaf children, and improvements and standardization in the field of deaf education. State and federal laws such as the recently reauthorized IDEA give parents a means to secure improvements in their child's education, if the parent knows how to utilize the law. At the state level, legislation proposed earlier this year specified the certification of all educational interpreters by the year 2000. And, last but not least, RID has resumed focusing on educational interpreting.

Those of us who attended the recent RID National Convention in Long Beach had the opportunity to attend the NEIC 1st National Conference prior to the start of the convention. Daniel Burch addressed the need for RID to reach out to educational interpreters, and to provide leadership in defining the standards and the role of the interpreter in the educational setting. We look forward, in 1998, to seeing a professional standards paper on educational interpreting come into being. With the emergence of a newly energized EdITOR SIG group we have renewed strength.

We are feeling revitalized—and gearing up for ever continuing progress! ■

Mainstreaming Within a Residential School Program: The Best of Both Worlds

By James G. Virgilio, CI and CT, BA, Louisiana

VIEWS, Vol. 15, Issue 2, February 1998, Page 10

In the field of Deaf Education, there has long been a debate over whether students who are deaf should be mainstreamed into the public schools or placed at a residential school for deaf children. Supporters of mainstreaming, or inclusion, contend (among other things) that the public school can meet the academic needs of the deaf student, while giving him or her the opportunity to learn how to live in a "hearing world." Supporters of residential programs contend (among other things) that the "school for the deaf" meets the deaf student's academic needs in an environment where communication happens freely and naturally (in sign language). At the Louisiana School for the Deaf, students have the opportunity to take courses in local public schools as part of their academic program at LSD. This option, which also occurs at other residential schools, offers Deaf students the best of mainstreaming while maintaining the best of the Deaf School experience.

LSD has been offering mainstream courses since 1979, through a cooperative agreement with the East Baton Rouge Parish School System (EBR) and the local vocational-technical institute. In a meeting to develop the student's Individualized Education Plan (IEP), parents, teachers, school staff, and the students, when appropriate, come together to make choices about courses the student will take during the academic year. Mainstreaming for one or more classes is an option when the course(s) the student needs is not offered at LSD, or when the course at the public school offers a challenge or is considered the best placement for that particular student. Examples of such courses include vocational courses, honors academic courses, Gifted and Talented program courses, and art courses. Students must also meet the following criteria to participate in the mainstreaming program:

A. The student agrees to participate actively in the program.

B. The student functions at or about the grade level of the receiving class.

C. The student possesses the appropriate receptive and expressive communication skills.

D. The student possesses sufficient self-confidence, positive self-concept and image, and social and emotional maturity commensurate with the level of the receiving class.

E. Parents agree to the student's participation and take an active and supportive role.

The Coordinator of the Sign Language / Interpreting Services at LSD makes arrangements with EBR to determine the most appropriate mainstreaming site. Once a site is determined and classes are scheduled, the SL/IS Coordinator then assigns LSD's full-time educational interpreters for the academic year. LSD may utilize contracted interpreters as necessary and if qualified. LSD's staff interpreters are required to have at least a Level IV State Certification or have at least CI or CT certification from RID.

While taking mainstream courses, the deaf student learns how to use interpreter services appropriately.

The deaf student interacts directly with his or her hearing peers and with the teacher. The hearing students and the teacher are exposed to Deaf Culture and also learn how to use interpreter services through their interaction with the deaf student. The deaf student may explain something to a hearing student because he or she didn't get it but the deaf student did. He or she may work with a hearing peer on a class project. The teacher and the deaf student may discuss last night's homework. The deaf student may listen to all the crosstalk when no one is supposed to be talking.

The interpreter is the liaison between the mainstream teacher and LSD. Because he or she is a member of the education team responsible for academic progress, the interpreter reports the student's progress (e.g., test scores, achievements, difficulties) to the SL/IS Coordinator, who then forwards that information to the LSD Principal and appropriate supervising teacher. The student's grades from mainstreaming are included with his or her regular report card from LSD.

Sometimes the placement is found to be inappropriate, and the IEP team reconvenes to reconsider the placement. The placement is not considered unsuccessful, because everyone involved, from the deaf student to the public school teacher, learns a great deal even in a short time. Such a lesson occurred last fall at LSD when it was determined that the elementary school class into which two deaf students were mainstreamed was indeed *too* elementary and wasn't meeting the students' needs. LSD has since developed an accelerated program for those two students.

The Louisiana School for the Deaf has adopted the motto, "Kids Come First." As part of its ongoing efforts to ensure its students have a well-rounded education sufficient for the student to succeed in the transition from school to college or from school to work, LSD offers the opportunity to gain access to what is available in the public schools without giving up the academic programs and opportunities for social and linguistic development that a residential school offers. Students in the mainstream program are successful in the "hearing world," and show the hearing world what deaf students can do. These students are able to take full advantage of the social and extra-curricular programs at LSD: sports, after school activities, Junior NAD, and other clubs, in addition to their on-campus classwork. They continue to learn about Deaf Culture and their place within that culture. As the mainstreaming vs. residential school debate continues, perhaps LSD and similar schools for the deaf can be resources for those in education to see that deaf education doesn't have to be "either-or," but may be the best of both. ■

So You Want to Change the System? Work in School!

By Toni Rees, Associate, Maine

VIEWS, Vol. 15, Issue 2, February 1998, Page 12

Who can combat ignorance and naivete in public schools? You, with certification, the best and most experienced interpreters who can hardly bring yourselves to read this edition of *VIEWS*!

Today there is a call from an elementary school on my voice mail that I cannot bear to answer, so I write this instead! You face these questions too. From a teacher, "A little deaf girl is coming to my class next week. How do I get ready for her..." And yesterday's question, "How do I get certified as an educational interpreter now that I have finished both adult education ASL classes?" Take a breath. Does your stomach knot? Do you choose to give simplistic answers that don't reveal the complexity? Do you refuse to struggle through explanations one more time? Let me tell you my strategies and reasons for them.

1. Have on hand brochures or other material to send (Some resources are listed at the end of this piece.) Why? Because the caller/questioner will only half understand or remember what I say. Words on paper reinforce and expand understanding and take the pressure off me.

2. Organize or keep attending meetings with Deaf professionals, service providers, and interpreters, to draft, lobby for, and pass legislation to require minimal standards for interpreters in your state.

3. Prepare stock responses to frequently asked questions so you can give answers without unbearable emotional anguish and get through the day upholding your values and beliefs. For example, the call I really do have to make in a few minutes is to an elementary school where several teachers and tutors want to enroll in an interpreting class that begins next week. The telephone message says they all know "some signs". Project what they probably believe: a) any fool can learn to sign easily and quickly, b) interpreting is easy, c) the academic and social needs of deaf children can best be met in public school classrooms. Where do you start connecting with their world experience? The easiest assumption to challenge is a) the fact that learning another language is difficult. Most people have struggled with learning Spanish or another modern language and you point out that learning ASL is similarly hard. For b) and c) I mail a brochure and guide developed with Maine RID and refer them to a couple of contacts.

This is where the soul searching kicks in. Am I, are you, perpetuating a system that you believe is harming children? Have you thought through your values, beliefs, and convictions? I am an educator who prepares teachers to work with children from kindergarten through grade 12, and I am also an interpreter and coordinator of classes for interpreters. I know: a) learning a language as an adult is excruciatingly difficult, b) becoming a competent interpreter requires tremendous ongoing effort, and c) deaf children experience horrible isolation and limited access to education in public schools.

In the face of these facts, what are your, or my, options? One extreme says "refuse to work in or with public schools". The other response is that deaf children are in, and will remain in, public schools with or without competent interpretation services. So are our choices similar to aide workers facing a famine in Ethiopia? In other words, do we say we should not pour aid into Ethiopia as we only perpetuate a bad situation where the land and political system cannot equitably sustain the population? This central ethical question confronts all who face complex choices every day. Do we act to support our convictions? Is averting our eyes from a famine an ethical option? Imagine if the very best interpreters agreed to spend one year in public schools. What might change? How would teachers and educational administrators change their thinking and actions in light of best interpreting practices? Ask yourself the opposite question. If the very best interpreters refuse to work in schools, what impact does that have? The hard reality we know is that beginning interpreters with the least preparation tend to work in schools. Beginning interpreters have not yet developed the values, beliefs, and convictions that enable a person to confront a system. Beginning interpreters do not have the knowledge base and competencies to assuredly demonstrate the possibilities and limitations of interpreting in schools.

What is the point? Are we going to moan and feel bad for deaf children isolated in schools? Or are we going to get down and dirty inside public school classrooms? Now I am going to return that telephone call to the elementary school. Thank you for reading. I welcome your comments, Toni Rees, University of Southern Maine (tonirees@usm.maine.edu).

Resources

ASL-English Interpretation in Educational Settings [brochure] and Sign Transliteration in Educational Settings [brochure] (1997). Portland, ME: Maine RID/University of Southern Maine.

Interpreters for the Deaf: Roles and responsibilities in educational settings (1997). Portland, ME: Maine RID/University of Southern Maine.

Florida Department of Education. (1986). Interpreting in the Educational Setting. Tallahassee, FLA: Bureau of Education Technical Assistance Paper #12.

National Association of State Directors of Special Education . (1994). Deaf and Hard of Hearing Students: Educational service guidelines. Alexandria, VA.

National Task Force of Educational Interpreting. (1989). Educational Interpreting for Deaf Students. Rochester, NY: National Technical Institute for the Deaf.

∎

Interpreting With Deaf Preschoolers

By Cindy Affonso, Associate Member, QA II, Michigan

VIEWS, Vol. 15, Issue 2, February 1998, Page 14

For the interpreter who is not familiar with the *Educational* Interpreters Code of Ethics *(EDITORS NOTE: RID has only one official Code of Ethics, which applies to all members. What is being referred to here is a presentation by two RID members at the 1985 RID Convention.)*, interpreting for preschoolers is a drastic departure from the normal role of Interpreter.

The role of the preschool interpreter is a very mixed one. At one moment you are interpreter, next teacher, then aide, or even bathroom helper to the preschooler. Your role can be very confusing. There really is no defined role for the interpreter at this young age. The key is flexibility. You are the main source of language for the student. In order to give the widest variety of language examples to the student you need to be involved in all areas of their school experience. That means sitting with them at the table during snack or lunch or, showing them good manners by your example and explaining; "Don't reach in front of Sally for the bread, please ask Sally to pass it to you."

My experience has shown that the student will cling to you as their safe haven. You are the only one in the classroom that gives them undivided attention. Be careful here!!! Even though you need to be actively involved in all aspects of their school experience, you also have the added responsibility of encouraging the child to reach out to others, to interact and foster friendships. The child may see you as their own personal playmate and demand the undivided attention that they have become accustomed to. It is at this point that you will need to step back (physically and emotionally) and encourage the student to play with others or better yet, ask others if they would like to play animals, look at books or swing together with your student.

Although the role of interpreter is very broad at this age level, it is still important that you remember your main responsibility is to interpret. A preschooler will probably not understand that you are the "interpreter" and that you voice for them. As you model the interpreter's role, the child will learn early on, through you, their language.

YOU are the student's *main* source of their language. I can't emphasize enough the importance of the preschool interpreter having a wide and varied vocabulary. This does *not* mean having attended a few sign classes.

Some school administrators and well-meaning individuals that know sign language may think that a limited knowledge of sign language by the interpreter is acceptable at this young age. After all, at this age it's mostly—line up, sit down, wash your hands, pay attention, don't touch, etc... right? Wrong! It's true that those are consistent daily commands, but what of language development and acquisition? This young student's language level and vocabulary will be a direct reflection of the level and vocabulary of the interpreter. Brenda Seal, in *"Best Practices in Educational Interpreting,"* tells us that "these earliest years are special in that children are most successful—perhaps even neurologically programmed to be successful-in acquiring the language or languages of their environment and/or culture."

How can you expect a young preschooler to learn ASL from an interpreter who barely knows it themselves? It's an awesome responsibility to be teaching a little one their language. And teach we do! That's why we need the best interpreters for our youngest clients. At this young age they will pick it up very quickly. We want to make sure that what they are learning is being signed correctly (sign production), accurately (concept-oriented) and with correct facial and mouth movements.

Each day, as you interpret, you will be using new signs and concepts that the student does not know or recognize. It will be part of your responsibility to teach these new signs/concepts to the student after the normal instruction is finished. Usually during play time is the best. You naturally can't teach all of them at once. Pick one or more that seem to be connected with a theme in the classroom at the time. (ie: Fire prevention week; alarm, fire, fireman, hose etc.) What seems to work best? Repeat, repeat, repeat! But the repetition must be accompanied with a wide variety of examples. Don't be afraid to go about the classroom, finding examples of "shiny"; tin foil, the sun on your ring or other metal object, another student's metal hair clip, a book with metallic pictures (Rainbow Fish is great!). Don't be afraid to use props from around the classroom; a doll to illustrate "ignore" to another doll, or a stuffed animal to illustrate "refuse" when another animal asks it to do something. It may be more helpful to use stuffed or toy animals while teaching negative concepts. A preschooler may not understand that you are trying to *teach* "ignore". They may see your facial expressions and body language and feel that you are mad at them or don't want to be their friend any more.

It helps a great deal if you reintroduce the new sign in the context of a class project, story book or other activity that shows it's meaning. If this is not possible be ready to find, or better yet, explore the classroom with your student to find examples; "Where black?, Show me red., Two of us search for shiny, where?" Make it fun! If your student does not sign back to you at first, don't panic. They are learning it nonetheless. As they become comfortable with it, they will respond.

Get the whole class involved with a "Sign of the Week". That way everyone is learning sign along with your client. Even during "side" communications such as snack time or recess, involve whatever children are around in learning the new sign that you are teaching or emphasizing at that time. Be conscious of teachable moments. They often happen when we least expect them. Run with it!! Go where the interest of the student is focused. The attention span at this age is rather short. You may have to put aside what you had planned and focus on another concept. That's ok. You can always come back to your original plan at another time.

Your student will most likely have acquired the habit of pointing to what they want. As they increase their sign vocabulary you'll have to insist that they use their signs instead of pointing. If the child wants help, have them sign it. If the child wants milk, have them sign it. Like any young child, your student too, will try to get away with what they think they can! It's been documented how children will live up to the expectations set for them. Make sure your expectations are higher than theirs.

Try to refrain from assisting the children with their coats, backpacks and tying shoes. If you set that precedent at the beginning of the year you will not be overwhelmed with requests for help (from the students and teachers) especially when you should be interpreting. It's hard to say no to these little faces but

you can respond with:

"Mrs. _____ will help you."
"I'm working right now."
"I need my hands for sign language right now."
"Please wait for Miss _____, she'll help you"
"Go ask Mrs. _____, she is free right now."

If hearing aids are acquired during the preschool years be sure to show them to the class and explain why they are used. Children (and adults) are afraid of the unknown. Make sure your class has as much knowledge as possible about deafness to help them become comfortable and accepting of you and your client.

Communication with the teacher is of the utmost importance. The regular teacher obviously cannot teach sign but you are not to usurp the regular teacher's role. Discuss with the teacher what you plan to do and how you will do it.

Not only is communication with the teacher important but also vital is the shared communication with the parents at home about the new signs that their child is learning. As you focus on a new sign or concept, copy it from a sign book and send it home with your student. Keep a list of the signs you are working on and see if it is possible to meet with the parents to show them how to correctly make and use the signs that their child is learning. Conference time may be a good time to do this if no other time is available.

You may also be asked to list the child's receptive and expressive concepts for Individualized Educational Program (IEP) purposes. If you are already listing new vocabulary used, just add to it. Then the teacher and the Teacher Consultant will have the information available to help in their decision making process. You (and they) may just be surprised at how much language your student has acquired!

At this young age any adult in the classroom is considered a "teacher". It is important that you listen to the

children (as well as interpret) but be careful not to fall into the trap of disciplinarian. All the children, including your Deaf child, need to know where the power lies in the class. When children do come to you (and they will) with tattles and problems be sure to *listen* and *respond* with such answers as:

"Be sure Mrs. (teachers name) knows about that"
"Go tell Mrs. _____ right now. She'll want to know."
"I'm sorry that happened. Does Mrs. _____ know about that?"
"That hurt your feelings, I'm sorry."
"It wasn't nice for so and so to say/do that. Mrs. _____ needs to know what he/she did".

Children of all ages need to know that if they go to an adult with a problem they will be heard. Do not "just interpret" and ignore the child. The feeling of school being a safe place BEGINS at this level. We don't want to destroy or impede that. When you respond with a warm caring attitude you not only encourage the classroom child but your own client as well.

What a tremendous honor and responsibility it is to be in such a position of influence on these young children. Do your best!! Work in PARTNERSHIP with the classroom teacher, aides and parents. Look to other interpreters for advice and feedback.
Attend workshops and conferences of all kinds but especially Educational Interpreter Workshops. The state of Michigan Department of Education funds an Educational Interpreters Workshop Series every Fall and Spring at Michigan School for the Deaf and Blind in Flint. Check out your State Department of Education and see if they offer anything similar.

We need the best interpreters for our youngest clients so they may grow into adults with a rich language. And only your commitment to making yourself the best you can be will make that happen! ■

Stuck Between a Rock and a Hard Place

By Carlos Budding, Associate, District of Columbia

VIEWS, Vol. 15, Issue 2, February 1998, Page 16

In November of 1997, I attended a silent weekend in Richmond, Virginia. Sponsored by RMVRID, the silent weekend boasted an invaluable group of Deaf presenters who did their best to both enlighten, educate, and entertain us. One distinguished figure, Rachel Bavister, Principal of the Virginia School for the Deaf and Blind in Staunton, spoke to a group of interpreters regarding educational interpreting and the mainstream setting. Titled "Between a Rock and a Hard Place", the focus of her presentation dealt with two issues; first, the dichotomous relationship as both Principal of a residential school and as an instructor of educational interpreters. Secondly, she discussed the struggle between a deaf child's independence and a hearing world's good intentions. Her presentation serves as the catalyst for this commentary.

My intentions are also twofold: first to discuss the nebulous nature of the RID Code of Ethics (COE) as applicable to the educational setting; and second, to address my feelings associated with stepping out of its rigid boundaries.

The foggy nature of the COE has been a problem from the beginning of my training and has continued to this day. From the onset, I have confronted conflicting messages regarding the COE in the mainstream. "What the code says and what we do is sometimes different", I remember a professor saying. When I took my Quality Assurance and Screening (QAS) written test, the proctor stated, "When answering the questions, think about the COE in its purest form and don't be influenced by what you might have done in the past." There appears to be an unwritten code, a common knowledge shared by many, that the COE does not always apply

in this field. This concept is further supported when discussing issues with colleagues. It seems that at one point or another, educational interpreters have either confronted and/or struggled with COE issues as they apply to the educational field. Few solutions exist to the problems educational interpreters confront. Instead, interpreters are left with a sense of unease, focusing intensely on the task at hand and praying hard that nothing out of the ordinary happens.

To illustrate my second point, I borrow a story told by Ms. Bavister. It is the story of a young man and a little bird. Ms. Bavister used it to represent the (sometimes uneasy) relationship between the deaf and hearing consumers in the educational setting. I found her story to be an eye-opener. I use it to illustrate perhaps a counter point, an illumination on my feelings when I step outside of the COE.

One day, a young man discovered an injured little bird—a broken leg it seemed. Being the Samaritan that he was, the young man helped out the little bird. He took it home and spent many weeks nurturing the little bird back to full health. He fed it, gave it water, kept it warm, all with the hope that one day the little bird would get better. One day, when the little bird had gotten better, the man thought about releasing it. But the thought made him sad. He realized that by releasing it, he would be left alone. He thought about everything he had done for the little bird, how good it made him feel taking care of it. With a sense of trepidation, the man opened the door to the cage, slowly inserted his hand inside, but instead of letting it go, he broke the bird's other little leg. In the end, it was

more important for the young man, the caretaker, to feel good than for the little bird's freedom.

As a result of her story, I have begun to see myself in a different light. Suddenly, I envision my actions and deaf children as those analogous to the young man and the little bird. Furthermore, I find myself in heated mental debates, usually while in the middle of interpreting, evaluating and reevaluating my every decision as to its conduciveness or gravity in the interpreting process. For example:

Teacher is presenting wrong information. "Oh my gosh, this is so wrong! What should I do? COE says to do nothing, but something inside of me is telling me otherwise. Maybe interpret it in a way that would get the kid to ask a question. Hello?! When was the last time the kid raised his hand? Maybe just present the right information. But then is that being unfair to the other hearing children? Wait a minute, whom am I here for?"

Material is verbose or confusing. "Here we go again. What's the point here? Is he trying to put all the kids to sleep? The kid isn't getting it. Maybe I can bring it down a notch or two. But wait, is that following with the intent of the speaker?

Subject deals with an event the child is not aware of. "Seems like Bobby (fictitious name) didn't watch TV last night. I wish he would raise his hand and ask about what we're talking about. But he told me he feels dumb when he asks a question. Maybe if I tangent for a moment I can clue him in. Can I do this?"

While interpreting, student begins a conversation. "Bobby is talking to me about his little red wagon, and this would apply to long division how? Can I just tell Bobby to be quiet and pay attention while I'm interpreting, or is that stepping out of my role?

Interpreter and student have down time. "Test is over, and I forgot my most recent RID *VIEWS*. Bobby looks lonely again. I want to ask him what he plans on doing over the holidays. Can I do this, or does this break some code?"

In all the above instances, I have deviated from the rigid COE. The internal struggle between the RID COE and my own COE continues, and what determines stepping out of role or code, depends on outside circumstances (i.e. is the child paying attention, do I have time to explain, what mood the child or I am in). In the past, when having stepped out for whatever reason, the initial guilty reaction was quickly extinguished when witnessing the child understanding the concept. But now I wonder if I am doing the right thing.

In the end, I want what is best for the child. I side-step the discussion of the effectiveness of mainstreaming because it is a factor I cannot control. However, once the decision has been made, and the child is placed in my hands, my concern is providing him/her with the best interpreting that I can. Sometimes that means stepping out of my role or code. But in light of Ms. Bavister's presentation, the line between doing what I think is best, and becoming like the man with the bird is smudged. And like Ms. Bavister, I too feel stuck between a rock and a hard place. ∎

Ethics In Educational Interpreting

By Elizabeth A. Winston, TC. Ph.D, Oregon

VIEWS, Vol. 15, Issue 2, February 1998, Page 30

As I travel around the US, meeting with educational interpreters, presenting workshops on educational interpreting, and consulting with educators of the deaf, I often hear discussions about the applicability of the RID Code of Ethics to educational interpreting. Of course, for years there has been hot debate over whether the RID Code of Ethics applies to educational interpreting. But as I listen to the debate and the arguments, I sometimes find a more disturbing argument beneath. Sometimes, it seems that applying the RID Code of Ethics is irrelevant to these debates. The underlying question is not, "Does the RID Code of Ethics work here?" but rather, "Do I need to have any ethics at all if I work in an educational system? They pay me, they tell me what to do and I should do it. I can't have ethics if they don't want me to."

Hmmm, this argument has been used often in the past, and world opinion has consistently found it to be unacceptable. After WW II, Nazis were found guilty of atrocities — exterminating millions because "The boss told me to do it!" The excuse, the shirking of human responsibility, was not to be tolerated!

Let me present a scenario—Dr. Welby is a well-known physician, greatly admired for diagnosing health problems and finding cures- whether they be surgical, medicinal, nutritional or emotional. He is renowned for helping people move from illness to health.

Upon retirement, Dr. Welby is not ready to give up practicing medicine entirely. He accepts the position of a visiting doctor at a hospice care nursing center. The Center has two missions — care for sick patients and earn a profit.

One day, Patient Jones is admitted to the Center. After tests and observation, Dr. Welby discovers that Patient Jones has an operable tumor. With an operation, Patient Jones could be cured, moving from a life of progressively debilitating pain and eventual death, to a life of health and wellness.

What is the choice here? Do you think it is obvious? Is it obvious that Dr. Welby will choose to recommend the operation to make this change in Patient Jones' life? Would you be outraged if Dr. Welby considered any other decision/action?

My guess is that you would be incensed!

Let me propose other options— after all, Dr. Welby is now paid by the Center. And remember, they have two missions — take care of sick patients and earn a profit.

1. Dr. Welby has been told to take care of sick patients. Recommending that Patient Jones have the operation means that she will no longer be sick. He can't recommend the operation or he will be in violation of the Center's "ethics" — he is supposed to take care of sick patients, not cure them. (and, if he keeps curing patients, won't he risk losing his job???) He chooses to keep on "caring" for Patient Jones, since that is what the Center has hired him to do.

2. Consider the second mission of the Center — earn a profit. The operation will be expensive and would not contribute to the profits of the Center. And, if the patient is cured by the operation, the Center's profits will decrease because they will lose a paying customer. Thus, recommending the operation is definitely against the Center's "ethics."

So, Patient Jones is left to die, slowly and painfully, because Dr. Welby is paid by the Center. He follows their dictates because they pay him and Patient Jones does not.

Outrageous? Unthinkable? Unacceptable? Yes! We expect professionals to adhere to their ethical beliefs because they are right, not because they are paid for by the highest bidder.

But, you may say, this is different. This scenario has to do with a life — a person living or dying. You can't compare it to me working as an interpreter and following the dictates of a school system! No one is dying here!

No? Ethically, what is the difference between choosing the slow and painful death of a body and choosing the slow and painful death of a mind? Refusal to act ethically as an educational interpreter because "someone else told me" is both outrageous and unacceptable. Allowing a mind to slowly wither and die because of a school's dictates is at best unethical; at worst it is an example of the child abuse so many believe occurs in mainstreaming.

There is no question that educational interpreters must behave ethically, regardless of the dictates of the "person with the money." Choosing a course of action based on money at the expense of ethics cannot be tolerated. As you participate in discussions about the applicability of the RID Code of Ethics the next time, I challenge you to assess the real argument — is it about *how* to behave ethically, or is it about *whether* ethics are relevant? Are minds dying in your school?

But, you say, you believe that professional ethics are important for educational interpreters. The dilemma is how do they apply to all the things that educational interpreters must do during the day?

I suggest that the confusion lies in the title, Educational Interpreter, and not in applying the Code of Ethics. A review of your job description, or of your daily assignments, may well show that you were not hired to be an interpreter, but rather to be an expert in providing educational access for deaf students.

If you think of yourself as an "interpreter," it becomes very confusing trying to apply guidelines of impartiality, confidentiality, and so on, especially when you have been assigned to monitor the playground. I recommend that you re-think your role, considering yourself an expert in providing accessibility rather than as an educational interpreter.

As an expert in providing educational access, there is no difficulty at all. As the accessibility expert, you have several different roles, each with different responsibilities. When you succeed in clearly defining and separating those roles, it is easy to see where the Code of Ethics applies to the role of interpreting. And, if you have been assigned playground duty (or tutoring duty, or aiding duty) you have responsibilities unrelated to the RID Code of Ethics during those roles.

It is only when you are assigned to interpret that the RID Code of Ethics is relevant to your decision making. If, as so often happens, you have several roles with the same student and teacher, you need to be very clear in your role definition. And you need to make sure that not only you understand the roles, but that the others do, too (isn't this the essence of behaving professionally?). And that they understand, clearly, that when your role calls for you to interpret you must follow the RID Code of Ethics.

But who decides which role you have when? Probably when you were first hired the school made some

arbitrary decision without an understanding of the impact interpreting has on an education. Or, as is more often the case, no one has ever thought about defining and separating your roles. Until now!

But, who are you to define your own roles? Just the interpreter, just the hired help?

No! You are a member of the educational team, and you have contact with the student in many different capacities. When asked about a situation in which you tutor, you respond with information about the tutoring situation—what you tutor, how you tutor, how the teacher provides you with direction in the tutoring, and how the student responds to the tutoring. When asked about a fight on the playground that occurred when your were monitoring the playground, you report the events as a playground monitor.

And, when asked about **an interpreted event**, you provide input about how **interpreting** affects the accessibility of that event. Because, you ARE the only person who has contact with the student all day, every day as an interpreter and you are the ONLY person in the setting who sees, clearly and consistently, when, where, and how interpreting provides (and does not provide) accessibility to an education. You are the only person who can address these issues in most schools.

But, you say, the team doesn't ask me about interpreting, they ask me about teaching and learning. Yes, of course they do. They have no training about interpreting — they have little idea about the tremendous impact that interpreting has on the access to an education. They do not know which questions to ask you, the expert in accessibility. They do not understand that you are NOT a qualified teacher, that you are not qualified to test language acquisition, that you are not the panacea for the deaf student. You are, in your role as interpreter, the expert in providing access to someone else's expertise in the classroom when possible, and in analyzing those situations that do

not allow for adequate access.

You, as a professional interpreter, have a professional responsibility to educate the team about your areas of expertise (and to refrain from pretending to have expertise in areas where you do not have it!). It may be flattering to be asked for input where we are not experts — but responding to this flattery with unqualified input is deceptive and self-aggrandizing.

Let me describe another scenario — you, the expert in educational access for deaf students in the mainstream, are at the IEP meeting. You are there because you work with Susan, a deaf student. You are asked to report on her progress. Some common responses:

"I can't discuss Susan's progress because I am an educational interpreter and the RID Code of Ethics says it is wrong." Or, "Susan is doing great! She is getting A's and B's in most of her classes, she never skips class, and I never have to tell her to pay attention."

The first response is neither professional nor, more to the point, effective. It is negative and passes judgment on the asker. We can not expect them to know our Code of Ethics nor to respect us for failing to participate as professionals. And by giving this response we have denied the team information that is vital to providing educational access to deaf children.

And the second response? At best deceptive, at worst gross malpractice. While it is true that we are often, by default, the person who has the most contact and communication with the student, this ongoing contact does not automatically turn us into experts in learning and teaching. We are, or should be, experts in interpreting. Yet, it is rare for me to hear "interpreters" offering information about interpreting — it seems so much more appealing to provide unqualified information about teaching and learning.

What might be an effective, professional response? A response that re-directs the question into more specific areas.

For example — "I work with Susan in several different capacities, and I will share with you what I can related to each."

"In Chemistry, I function as an aide in the classroom. In that capacity I work with all the students as well as Susan, and my work with her is the same as with other students. Ms. Peters (the teacher) provides me with directions and materials, and I work with any student who needs help. Ms. Peters will be able to tell you whether Susan is keeping up with the objectives of the class. As far as access to the information, most of the class happens through interactive CD ROM instruction on the computers. These programs are all written in English, and Susan has access to the information to the extent that she understands the English on the screen. She does not ask for this to be interpreted — Ms. Peters can comment about whether she appears to understand the lessons."

"In History, I function as the interpreter, where I transmit the teacher's information to Susan and vice-versa, and have no function as an aide or tutor. This class is accessible via interpreting about 90% of the time. At the beginning of the semester I analyzed the class for accessibility, both visual and linguistic accessibility, and found that the class itself was only about 50% accessible to Susan through interpreting. Mr. Allen (the teacher), Susan and I have worked together to make the class more accessible. Some of the changes have been:

changing the seating arrangements so that Susan sits in the back of the room. In this way she can see all the interaction of the class without constantly having to turn around and miss part of the interpreting. (The class was too big to consider arranging the desks in a semi-circle.)

Mr. Allen gives Susan a copy of his notes after each class. This allows Susan to focus on the interpretation rather than worry about taking notes. However, since note-taking serves a purpose in learning, Susan is not able to take advantage of the aid to memory that note-taking provides all the other students. Thus, this does not provide full access to the educational activity.

During demonstrations, Mr. Allen has changed his presentation style to accommodate visual access for Susan. Instead of talking while he demonstrates something, he usually describes the demonstration first, then lets the students watch it. This lets Susan have access to both the information and the visual aid. (When he talked and demonstrated at the same time, Susan had to choose between watching the demonstration and watching the interpretation — she always lost access to half of the activity.)

Areas that are still problematic — videotapes in class. When Mr. Allen shows a videotape, the other students watch the tape and listen to the information at the same time. Susan must choose which to watch, the tape or the interpreter. We have tried to work around this problem by letting Susan watch the tape before the class so that she can see the information, but this requires time away from other work. We also try to get captioned videotapes when possible. Since Mr. Allen does not show videotapes very often, the activity is a barrier to access only occasionally."

"Mr. Allen will be able to address whether Susan is progressing satisfactorily in his class."

These responses demonstrate a delineation of roles, an understanding of the type of input appropriate to each role, and a manner that is both effective and professional.

Conclusion

I challenge those who function in the role of interpreter, whether it is your primary role, or a portion of a multi-role position, to respect the goals of the RID Code of Ethics. I also challenge you, in your role as interpreter, to provide input that is related to interpreting — how interpreting provides access to an education, how interpreting is affecting the classroom, how and when interpreting provides access and how and when it poses barriers to access. These are the appropriate professional contributions of an interpreter. Define your roles, understand your responsibilities within each role, and participate as a team member within those boundaries.

Provide an environment where children's minds not only live, but flourish. ∎

Educational Interpreters Document Efforts to Improve

By Brenda C. Seal, Ph.D., CSC, Virginia

VIEWS, Vol. 16, Issue 2, February 1999, Page 1

Educational interpreters, like all other professional interpreters, are expected to grow in their knowledge, skills, and credentials. One of our ethical tenets holds that, because we value professional development, we actively seek to further our skills and knowledge (RID, 1995). For nationally certified interpreters, efforts to develop professionally or to "improve" can be documented in continuing education units (CEUs). The Certification Maintenance Program of RID enables us to report CEUs to the National Office where they are recorded, monitored, and maintained (see ACET, 1996; and Sullivan, 1996). This same type of documentation and verification of professional development is common to many professions and often represents the gauge by which advancement within the profession is measured.

This report is about educational interpreters who are *not* certified members of RID. These interpreters make up a large number of practicing interpreters and transliterators in our local schools. And while I do not endorse blanket approval of "unqualified" interpreters working in our schools, I recognize that these same interpreters should not be abandoned in our efforts to raise the status of educational interpreters nationwide. Indeed, I suggest that all nationally certified interpreters should support efforts to "improve" the credentials of educational interpreters who are "under-credentialed," either because of their underdeveloped skills or because of their lack of knowledge, skill, and experience. This report is about efforts to support a group of educational interpreters in Virginia as they worked to improve their skills and knowledge and to meet the regulatory credentials set by the Virginia Department of Education.

Method

Forty-three participating interpreters from 17 different school systems across Virginia were selected as part of a research project sponsored by the state Department of Education. The goal of the project was to determine if these 43 interpreters who had not met the state's regulation (national certification or Virginia Quality Assurance Screening [VQAS] Level III in either interpreting or transliterating by the third year of their anniversary) could raise their credentials as a result of different intervention approaches.[1] The 43 interpreters were selected because they responded to "a call" (letters and phone calls to all the school systems in Virginia reporting the employment of educational interpreters) and agreed in writing to the conditions of their year-long participation. Eleven of these 43 interpreters were randomly assigned to Group 1; these interpreters received site visits by nationally certified interpreters who observed them as they interpreted and made recommendations for improvement. Group 1 interpreters also provided a sample videotape of their interpreting that was analyzed for "equivalence" between source and target languages. Another 11 interpreters were randomly assigned to Group 2; these interpreters participated in a testing workshop that focused on how to reduce test anxiety and maximize test performance. A videotaped performance during a mock test that simulated the VQAS was also analyzed and recommendations were offered by the same nationally certified interpreters who had made site visits to the Group 1 interpreters. The third group of interpreters, Group 3, received both interventions—the personal site visits and videotape analysis, the testing workshop and videotape analysis, and recommendations for improvement. Group 4 interpreters served as a control group; they received no intervention at all. All 43 interpreters were asked to keep records of the activities they engaged in during the course of the project and to rate, on a one-to-ten scale, the perceived value of those activities in improving their interpreting. Forty of the 43 interpreters reported their activities each month, from October through May. These 40 interpreters reported a total of 4,560 hours across the eight months, with no statistical difference in number of hours reported within either of the four groups ($F(34, 3) = .954$, $p > .05$). A look at the monthly data reported in Table 1 shows that November was the most active of the months: the interpreters reported a total of 1,102 hours. In contrast, March and May were the two lowest activity months with only 323 hours reported during March and 312 during May.

Analyses of the monthly data involved two statistical procedures: first, the coded data were entered for each interpreter into an SPSS data file that yielded summary statistics across all interpreters and all categories. Then, correlation coefficients were calculated between the number of hours per category and the average values the interpreters had placed on each activity. For example, the number of hours spent in a formal interpreting class were correlated with the value placed on that activity for all reporting interpreters.

Correlation coefficients were then subjected to significance testing and ranked from those that represented the highest positive relationships to those that represented the lowest negative relationships.

Results

Results of these analyses yielded several findings. Table 2 reveals the various activities reported by the interpreters from October through May and the average number of hours devoted to each activity. Activities that were reported by fewer than five interpreters or totaled less than 5 hours across the months were dropped from the statistical analysis. One of these, "Site Visit by Certified Interpreter," was reported by four interpreters for a total of 4 hours.

The average total hours reported across all interpreters for all activities combined was 88 hours (s.d. = 75). When each of the activities was compared across groups, only one activity statistically set the groups apart (F (3, 33) = 123.36, $p < .01$) — teaching sign language classes. One interpreter in Group 1 reported 5.5 hours per month teaching sign language; three in Group 2 reported 4.67 hours per month; two in Group 3 reported 7.25 hours per month; but one interpreter in Group 4 reported 25 hours per month devoted to teaching sign language classes.

A negative correlation coefficient, albeit very small and not statistically significant ($r = -.021$, $p > .05$), was calculated between the number of years of experience the interpreters reported and the number of hours they devoted to these activities. The interpreters reported an average of 6.25 (s.d. = 4.38) years in educational interpreting. (There was no statistical difference across the four groups in their years of experience; F (29, 3) = .492; $p > .05$.) As might be expected, those interpreters who reported more experience tended to report slightly less time working to improve their interpreting than interpreters new to the profession. A positive correlation, also very small and also not

statistically significant ($r = .09$, $p > .05$), between the interpreters' VQAS scores and the number of hours they reported working to improve their interpreting suggests that those with higher scores tended to report only slightly more hours each month than those with lower scores.

Table 3 provides correlation coefficients representing the relationships between the number of hours the interpreters devoted to an activity and the perceived value of that activity. Positive correlation coefficients indicate that the more time spent in an activity, the more valuable that activity was perceived by the interpreter to be in improving skills. Negative correlation coefficients indicate that the more time spent in the activity, the less valuable the interpreters perceived the activity in improving their skills.

Three of these activities, interacting with deaf people, watching self on videotape, and working on vocabulary, received the highest ratings or values from the interpreters. Five others—interpreting in the community; attending workshops and conferences; observing teachers, students, and classes; watching videotapes on sign language; reading print materials—were also judged by the interpreters to be valuable but not as valuable as the first three. Two other activities, interacting with other interpreters and attending classes on sign language or interpreting, carried high values as profitable, but negative correlation coefficients. Teaching sign language and observing interpreters were rated of moderate value but yielded negative correlation coefficients. These findings suggest a learning curve—that at the onset (perhaps the onset of a class or of the school year or of a relationship with other interpreters), educational interpreters value the learning they gain, but at some point during that course or during the year or during the relationship, the benefits plateau.

Discussion

These results are considered important for a variety of reasons

and to a variety of audiences. Most importantly, because of the competitive funding of this research grant, the results were submitted to the Virginia Department of Education with recommendations to continue sponsorship of activities designed to improve educational interpreters' skills and knowledge and to assist them in meeting the state's VQAS Level III or higher regulation. Virginia's status, like that of many states, is that the need for "qualified" educational interpreters far exceeds the number of available interpreters who hold the required national or state credentials. Continuing efforts to upgrade the status of these interpreters is critically important to the education of our deaf and hard-of-hearing students. Secondly, the results were shared with the 40 participating interpreters, those who took time each month to record their activities and to rate the activities for their perceived value. A comprehensive report was submitted to these interpreters with gratitude for their willingness to share their activities for analyses. The results have also been shared in four different forums: with the five nationally certified interpreters who serve as site visitors/consultants on the continuation of the project during this 1998-99 school year, with the 1998-99 administrators of educational interpreting grants in Virginia's schools, with a conference audience (South Carolina Registry of Interpreters for the Deaf Annual Convention), and with a workshop audience (Tidewater Community College Interpreter Training Workshop in Norfolk).

In each of these forums, the results have been discussed to reflect these points:

- The educational interpreters who participated in this project spent a considerable amount of time across a wide number of activities to improve their knowledge and skills and in hopes of meeting the credentialing requirements set by the state of Virginia. Most of their time, particularly in the fall months, was devoted to observing teachers and students and classes. Considerable time was also devoted to their own course work on interpreting, to interacting with deaf individuals, attending workshops, meetings, conferences, and so on.

- When the educational interpreters rated the value of their activities in improving their skills and knowledge, several activities stood out as being more helpful than others. Most striking of all the correlations was the finding that the more time spent in improving vocabulary, the more valuable it was perceived by the interpreters. Discussion of this result with the various audiences reported above raised several reflections: one, the vocabulary used in the educational setting can be overwhelming in its diversity and complexity. Secondly, interpreters must be constantly vigilant in determining how best to represent that vocabulary so that access to the language is maximized. An interpreter's ability to balance fingerspelling and invented signs and synonymous signs is only as successful as the interpreter's working knowledge of the vocabulary used in each algebra, civics, vocational, English, literature, science, physical education, music, history, geography, spelling, computer, psychology, sociology, etc., class in which he or she interprets.

- Interpreting in the community also ranked high in its investment potential. Discussion of this activity carries both negative and positive ramifications. Interpreters who have opportunities to interpret in their communities can grow immeasurably from their experiences. These same interpreters are at risk, however, of leaving the educational setting once they find security in community assignments. As a compromise, inter-

preter trainers and supervisors should encourage community assignments for learning that can be returned to or reinvested in the educational setting.

- Interpreters in this project spent little time in videotaping themselves but reported great value in doing so. Self-analysis, the zenith of any professional development activity, is highly facilitated when we step back and take a look at ourselves. Routine videotaping and observing videotaped performances for strengths and weaknesses and for changes over time is quite possibly the most valuable, yet least frequently accomplished activity we can engage in.

- Observing teachers, students, and classes at school; attending workshops and conferences; reading and studying print materials; interacting with deaf people; and watching videotapes on sign language are all valued by educational interpreters. However, the more time invested in these activities, the less valuable the activities become. Interacting with other interpreters, teaching sign language, attending classes on sign language or interpreting, and observing other interpreters actually have negative returns in their investment perceptions. These findings may be commonsense to seasoned interpreters who probably become more "intuitively selective" in their course and workshop choices over the years. Interpreters who teach sign language inside or outside their school systems are likely to agree that their learning curve advances more rapidly in the early stages of the school year or term than in the later stages, and in the first time the course is taught than in subsequent offerings. This does not imply, however, that a plateau in the learning curve is bad. It

merely suggests that one of our natural tendencies is to value most those learning experiences that show the most immediate boost or improvement in our learning. While the "timing" of teaching and learning has not yet been put to test, it appears from these findings that intense workshops, weekend courses, and immersion activities may be more advantageous than semester-long and year-long activities in impacting the direction of our learning curves. It may also be that brief interactions with a large number of deaf persons and a large variety of interpreters is more advantageous than interacting with the same deaf persons or same interpreters over a long period of time.

As indicated in the opening paragraph of this discussion section, these findings are considered important for a number of reasons and for a variety of audiences. One of the practical recommendations that might come from these results involves the timing of workshops, conferences, courses or videotaping. If the reports from these interpreters can be generalized to other educational interpreters, then we are all likely to choose November as the month to recommend any improvement activity. Discussion of this phenomenon is in order lest we abandon the other months of the year in our efforts to improve. Some of the audience feedback when I reported these findings focused on the "second" month of the project. It is possible that the participating interpreters were "psyched" about the project and more conscientious in their efforts to engage and report on improvement during the second month of the project. It may also be that November is psychologically viewed as the last big month before the holiday season sets in with its downward shift in learning activities. Whatever the reasons, testing these findings with other groups is appropriate before over-generalizing the results.

Another recommendation that comes from generalizing results would focus on devoting more time and attention to the vocabulary educational interpreters are expected to handle in their working day. Workshops in which interpreters share their signs for complex vocabulary, watch existing videotapes of technical signs, and expand with their own videotapes both within and beyond the school system should be important projects for systems that have sizeable interpreting staff.

Beyond these practical recommendations, I suggest that these findings are also useful to any of us who work as, sponsor, hire, supervise, or teach educational interpreting, and for many reasons—because of a personal desire to grow professionally, because of job security, or simply, because we may happen to love the idea of improving as educational interpreters.

References

Sullivan, S. (1996). ACET: New program for associate members encourages life-long learning. *RID VIEWS, 13,* 1, 24.

Cokely, D.

RID, Inc. (1995). Code of Ethics of the Registry of Interpreters for the Deaf, Inc. *RID Membership Directory.* Silver Spring, MD: RID Publications.

Sullivan, S. (1996). CMP update. *RID VIEWS, 13,* 30.

Acknowledgements

Gratitude is extended to the Virginia Department of Education for its sponsorship of this research grant, to each of the participating interpreters who contributed to these results, and to Shiree Harbick, research assistant who ran the final data.

[1] The report offered here is only a portion of a larger report on this research project that is still ongoing. ∎

Table 1. Monthly Activity Reported by Educational Interpreters

Month	Total Hours Reported
October	825
November	1,102
December	496
January	535
February	519
March	323
April	448
May	312
Total Hrs.	4,560

$x = 570$ per month

Table 2. Activities Reported Monthly (ranked from most to least frequent)

Activity	Average # Hours Per Month Devoted to Activity	(s.d.)*
Observing teachers, students, or classes (at school)	32.9 hrs.	(80.2)*
Attending a class on interpreting	26.6	(22.8)
Interacting with deaf individuals	24.8	(47.7)*
Attending workshops, meetings, or conferences	20.6	(14.9)
Interacting with other interpreters	15.8	(17.4)*
Observing other interpreters	13.0	(16.7)*
Reading/studying print materials on interpreting	9.6	(8.8)
Teaching sign language classes	9.5	(6.8)
Watching/studying videotapes on sign language/interpreting	8.4	(7.7)
Working on/developing vocabulary	6.9	(6.4)
Interpreting in the community	5.2	(4.5)
Critiquing/watching videotapes of self interpreting	2.8	(2.1)

Standard deviations (s.d.) represent the spread or deviations from the mean. Where the s.d. exceeds the mean, we can assume some extreme entries. For example, 3 interpreters in Group 1 reported a total of 22.5 hours in observing in the classroom, 1 in Group 3 reported only 6 hours, 2 in Group 4 reported a total of 32 hours, but 4 interpreters in Group 2 reported 268 hours observing in the classroom. Similar extremes are found in each s.d. asterisked.

Table 3. Average Rating of Interpreters' Activities and Relationships between Time Devoted to the Activity and its Perceived Value

Activity	Mean Rating	Correlation Coef. (r)
Working on/developing vocabulary	**8.25**	+ .75
Interpreting in the community	7.64	+ .38
Critiquing/watching self interpret on videotape	**8.53**	+ .354
Observing teachers, students, classes at school	7.25	+ .349
Attending workshops, conferences, meetings	7.42	+ .33
Reading/studying print materials on interpreting	6.84	+ .19
Interacting with deaf people	**8.58**	+ .18
Watching/studying videotapes on sign language	7.18	+ .12
Interacting with other interpreters	7.76	- .16
Teaching sign language	5.54	- .22
Attending a sign language or interpreting class	7.80	- .28
Observing other interpreters	6.59	- .33

None of the r values were statistically significant; $p > .05$ in all cases.

Ethical Educational Interpreting: Perspectives of Multiple Team Members

By SueAnne McCreery, Associate Member, AzIQAS V, M.ED;
Karen Feldman, MA; Heather Donnel, CI, BA; Kyra Davis, Arizona

VIEWS, Vol. 16, Issue 2, February 1999, Page 6

As is true with many other K-12 programs across the country, the Southeast Regional (SER) Cooperative is grappling with its definition of the role of the educational interpreter. SER prides itself, however, on its collegial practice of including all educational team members in defining this important function. This article will provide insight into the perspectives of multiple educational team members regarding the progress we are undergoing toward increased adherence to the RID Code of Ethics in the high school setting.

Coordinator's Perspective

When I was hired two years ago as SER's first interpreter coordinator, I encountered educational interpreters who regularly engaged in multiple roles with students. As an interpreter, I was uncomfortable with the ethical dilemmas often resulting from multiple roles. As a counselor, I had concerns about excessive student dependency. As a teacher, however, I recognized the significant developmental implications of interpreting with children. I also shared our teachers' concerns about the Deaf students' need for any and all linguistic input, given the communication barriers inherent in public school settings.

My perspective began to solidify, however, due to the work of Elizabeth Winston (1998). Winston acknowledged the reality of multiple roles when working in K-12 settings, but emphasized the importance of adherence to the RID Code of Ethics while engaged in the role of interpreting. Winston advocated a pragmatic, yet ethical approach to educational interpreting. As a result of Winston's

influence, I encouraged our educational interpreters to consider the ethical implications of their work.

It became readily apparent that our interpreters had been regularly disregarding two major tenets of the RID Code of Ethics in their efforts to meet the educational needs of their students:

Tenet 1 - Interpreters/Transliterators shall keep all assignment-related information strictly confidential.

Interpreters and teachers of the Deaf/Hard of Hearing were communicating daily about classroom content, students' understanding and behavior, and classroom teachers' objectives, etc.

Tenet 3 - Interpreters /Transliterators shall not counsel, advise, or interject personal opinions.

Interpreters were interjecting their own opinions daily in their efforts to tutor, reinforce teachers' lessons, redirect students, and/or meet their students' social needs.

In response to these concerns about confidentiality and neutrality, the educational team members at one of our high schools have risen to the challenge of creating an increasingly ethical educational interpreter role. After numerous and often painful meetings in which we hashed out the advantages and disadvantages of changing the status quo, the teacher of the Deaf/Hard of Hearing and the educational interpreters have agreed to increase confidentiality and neutrality through changing the role of the interpreter. Confidentiality: Interpreters are no longer expected to communicate with the teacher of the Deaf/Hard of

Hearing about academic-related information. The teacher of the Deaf/Hard of Hearing now obtains this information directly from students and/or classroom teachers. Neutrality: While interpreting in the classroom, interpreters will no longer also engage in tutoring or advising students. If and when tutoring is needed, arrangements will be made for this to take place outside of the regular classroom at a time when interpreting is not also required.

Teacher of the Deaf/Hard of Hearing's Perspective

During my first two years teaching Deaf students, I depended heavily on the interpreters that worked directly with my students. I expected the interpreters to facilitate communication in the classroom, to act as the liaison between the classroom teachers and myself, and to fill me in on information that I logistically could not obtain directly due to the large numbers of students in my caseload. While asking this of the interpreters conflicted with the confidentiality tenet of the Code of Ethics, I justified it by saying that we were on the same educational team and had a vested interest in our students' success. Admittedly, depending so much on the interpreters made my job easier.

Fast forward to August 1998. The beginning of my third year of teaching turned out to be one of the most difficult times of my career. I was approached by our interpreter coordinator to start thinking of our educational interpreters as people who solely facilitate communication in the classroom. This request sent a wave of stress through me. This year I would be working with 5 Deaf students, 5 educational interpreters, and approximately 38 classroom teachers. How would I possibly function without the interpreters acting as the liaison between the classroom teachers and me? How would the students succeed in their classes without the interpreters acting as the "middle men"? As I discussed this with our interpreter coordinator, we struggled to understand each other's perspectives. I was bound and determined to continue to have interpreters report to me and make my job easier. As I thought about it, however, I realized that this would be detrimental to the students. It was also a lot to ask of the interpreters to disregard the confidentiality tenet of the Code of Ethics.

Now that we have made it through a semester of change, I realize that everyone has benefited. I have had to arrange more time in my schedule to see classroom teachers on a regular basis. This has provided great opportunities for me to get into the classroom and not only see what's going on in class, but become more involved with the students, interpreters and classroom teachers. With interpreters no longer acting as liaison, the students have become more accountable for their education.

Educational Interpreter's Perspective

I am new to the interpreting profession, but I have seen enormous change occur over the past year where I am currently employed. The majority of this change is in regard to the neutrality tenet of the Code of Ethics. Last year, interpreters were expected to take on the role of tutor on occasion during class time. Because of the multiple roles played by the interpreters, the relationship between the classroom teachers and the students suffered, or worse, did not exist. Teachers were often unaware of their students' weaknesses because the interpreter was camouflaging or taking care of problems as they arose. The interpreter/tutor role also caused the students to develop a dependency on the inter-

preters for the "answers." The interpreter, a non-expert, was then inappropriately teaching the material. As a result, some incorrect information could have been taught.

Presently, tutoring has been taken out of the classroom and is now being provided by the classroom teacher, with the interpreter facilitating communication. This, of course, is an ideal situation and is often not possible. When the classroom teacher is unable to provide individual tutoring, the teacher of the Deaf/Hard of Hearing then reviews the information, with the interpreter serving as a tutoring resource. The last resort is for the interpreter to conduct the tutoring session. All of these situations now clearly occur outside of the regular classroom and this has greatly helped to clarify the role of the educational interpreter. This change toward a more neutral role has been a struggle. As interpreters, we sometimes feel that we know the subject better than the teacher or that we have a more effective way of teaching, but we know that we can not "counsel, advise, or interject our personal opinion." This can be a strain because none of us want to see our students fail. We've had to accept the idea that students sometimes need to fall on their faces in order to become more responsible to learn on their own.

Change has not come easily, but we all realize that a more neutral interpreter role will benefit our students in the long run. It will prepare them for their interactions with interpreters in college and in other adult settings. We recognize that we won't be there to tutor them, or break their falls, for the rest of their lives.

Deaf Student's Perspective

The situation with my interpreters last year was somewhat chaotic. My interpreter kept my teacher of the Deaf/Hard of Hearing on track about what was going on in my classes. My interpreter told her everything that was going on before I could tell her anything myself. I felt it was really my responsibility to inform my

teacher of everything. My interpreter would also tutor me before my tests and if I did bad on them, she'd encourage me to take them again.

This year is much different. The interpreters don't give information to my teacher of the Deaf/Hard of Hearing anymore. I'm starting to give my teacher more information myself now. My interpreters do not tutor me in class, so I must study by myself or ask for tutoring outside of class. These changes have made me feel more independene—independence is a good thing.

These changes with my interpreters have caused me to feel prepared for college. Now I feel more independent and can do anything I set out to do in college and in "the real world."

Summary

Implementing change toward more confidential and neutral educational interpreting practices has required the involvement and commitment of all educational team members. Michael Fullen's work has helped us understand that change inevitably involves a period of ambivalence, uncertainty, and ambiguity. Conflict and disagreement are fundamental to change. Despite the fact that change is a frustrating, discouraging undertaking, change is inevitable, while growth is optional. Our educational team members have chosen the course which we believe will help our students, and ourselves, grow to our fullest. ∎

The Implications for Deaf Children of The Individuals with Disabilities Education Act

By Ruth A. Sandefur, RSC, OIC:V/S, Kentucky

VIEWS, Vol. 16, Issue 2, February 1999, Page 8

With the advancement of the Individuals with Disabilities Education Act (IDEA), many Deaf and hard of hearing (those who need interpreting services) children are being mainstreamed in the public school education system. Many Deaf adults are intensely concerned, including the author of this article, who was educated in both the public school system and a residential school. Why are Deaf adults so concerned? Although we recognize some public school system administrators realize one of their responsibilities to Deaf and hard of hearing children is providing qualified interpreting services, there are still too many Deaf and hard of hearing children who have "interpreters" who can sign, but have been hired by the school administrators as teacher's aides. "Unfortunately, it is common for schools to make use of lesser-trained individuals who can be paid less than professional interpreters" (Marschark, pp. 121-122).

Deaf adults are not only concerned, though, because many school administrators are not hiring qualified interpreters. We are concerned about the information that is lost in the transfer between the teacher and the interpreter. There are numerous reasons for the breakdown in communication. According to Jack Levesque, hearing students only hear about 80% of the information offered them. "The other 20% might have been mispronounced, interrupted by other sounds, or somehow distorted" (DCARA). How about a Deaf or hard of hearing student who has an interpreter with a hearing teacher? According to Levesque again, let's say the interpreter gets 85% of what the teacher

says. He then turns around and presents this information to the student in sign language. Studies have shown that Deaf students actually receive less than 60% of what an interpreter signs. Why? There are many reasons. Sometimes the interpreter has misunderstood the teacher, but signs on, even though it doesn't make a lot of sense. Perhaps the light is glaring or the interpreter has on a wild print shirt, or the student in the next chair leans into her view, or the interpreter is not skilled or too slow, or the student stayed up late the night before and can't keep her eyes open. The list can go on and on (DCARA).

A third concern Deaf adults have is the feeling of isolation that many Deaf and hard of hearing children have experienced. This affects their self-esteem, among other social deficiencies that frequently occur among Deaf and hard of hearing children who are mainstreamed. At the residential schools, many "lifelong friendships are formed, where language and culture are learned, and where teaching can occur directly without the need for intermediaries such as interpreters" (Marschark, p. 115). Many of the "younger deaf children discover role models and an environment in which they are on an equal footing with their peers" (Ibid, p. 115).

This is not to imply "we can all wash our hands and go home." Instead, it shows how much our Deaf and hard of hearing children are missing when they are mainstreamed. It should be a challenge for interpreters in the public school system and considered a "wake-up call" that Deaf and hard of hearing children in mainstreaming programs deserve more than the services of a

competent, qualified interpreter to maximize access, integration, equality, and empowerment for everyone in this setting. "The role of an interpreter will vary dramatically depending on whether her/his clientele are children, youth, or adults" (Humphrey & Alcorn, p. 299). Humphrey & Alcorn also state that: *Minimally, interpreters in this setting should be graduates of an interpreter education program who have some course work in child development and education. Ideally, interpreters in educational settings should hold interpreter certification and a Bachelor's degree. This would generally insure that the individual hired can perform the interpreting/transliterating tasks required, has experience with formal educational (sic) her/himself, and has knowledge of and training in the special area of education.*

A fourth concern is that in mainstreamed programs, Deaf and hard of hearing students are frequently viewed from the negative, paternalist view of Deaf people instead of the "positive belief that Deaf people are members of a distinct cultural group" (Humphrey & Alcorn, p. 66). They stated: *This understanding leads to the view of Deaf individuals as normal, capable human beings who embrace life in a way different from other normal, capable human beings who are not deaf (Ibid, p. 66).* Humphrey & Alcorn "encourage interpreters to explore, understand and embrace" (p.67) this view of Deaf and hard of hearing students. They also recognize humor as a tool "used by members of the minority group to fight oppression" (p. 68). They suggest that a sense of humor "will help you in your journey into the culture and community of Deaf people" (p. 73).

They give examples of three jokes that Deaf people often use whenever they are referring to people "who have not yet demonstrated awareness or sensitivity to the needs and norms of the Deaf culture and community" (p. 74). According to Lane, Hoffmeister, & Bahan, "Deaf humor is frequently about oppression" (p. 157) and they use the example that Humphrey & Alcorn used about throwing a hearing passenger out the window because in their country there are plenty of hearing people. Humphrey & Alcorn warns interpreters to be aware of the power they have because they will find themselves in a very powerful position. They claim "we (interpreters) are all oppressors to one degree or another" (p. 74). According to Humphrey & Alcorn, interpreters "must determine to what degree you are an oppressor and deal with any oppressive tendencies, attitudes, beliefs, and behaviors you have before you are ready to begin interpreting" (pp. 74-75). They claim "the cycle of oppression can be broken" (p. 75) by functioning as allies who "supports, undergirds and foster d/Deaf individuals in their own struggle for liberation" (pp. 75 - 76).

Humphrey & Alcorn define "normalcy" and give excellent examples of the difference in normalcy between Deaf and hard of hearing individuals and hearing individuals. They mention the implications of cultural differences for interpreters and suggest "individuals can act/interact appropriately only if they have a frame or schema in place for a particular setting" (p. 83). Deaf adults believe as they do that "if you want to become an interpreter you must be fluent in two or more languages" (p. 84). They also mention if an interpreter wishes to work effectively with Deaf people (students) they "must be knowledgeable of and comfortable with the cultures of the language you use" (p. 84). Kirk & Gallagher, in their book *Educating Exceptional Children*, point out that it is important that Deaf and hard of hearing children "are not deficient or deviant;

they are simply children who cannot hear" (p. 311). They claim "It is far more productive to think of deafness as a sociological condition than a disease, to concentrate on the strengths of these children" (p. 311). They note that "cognition and language in dynamic interaction are two important factors in the learning process" (p. 312) for all children. They also note the "problems deaf children have with the English language, then impede their learning across all subject areas" (p. 312). They also mentioned that "most deaf children have difficulty developing linguistic skills because they have fewer opportunities to use English on a daily basis" (p. 312). Since Deaf children, whose parents are usually hearing, do not have models, "they cannot process the spoken word through hearing" (Kirk & Gallagher, p. 312).

It is imperative for interpreters to be conscious of all the problems that Deaf and hard of hearing children will encounter everyday due to all the problems that have been identified thus far. This author recommends that interpreters meet with the teachers a week before classes begin, if humanly possible, so that they can both discuss the problems Deaf and hard of hearing children encounter every day and discuss how they can resolve most of the problems together. All teachers should be aware that they will be the ones who will discipline any behavior problems that occur, but before she will be able to be fair with her Deaf and hard of hearing students she must be aware of the reasons they could occur. Hopefully, by identifying these problems in advance, most of the problems can be avoided. The interpreter might wish to suggest that the Deaf and/or hard of hearing students teach signs once or twice a week. As the Deaf and/or hard of hearing students teach signs, they will most likely feel they have some control over the problem of isolation, because as the hearing classmates learn signs, they will use them with the Deaf and/or hard of hearing students. There is a solution for every prob-

lem. The challenge is identifying the problem and solution.

Bibliography

Humphrey, Janice H. & Alcorn, Bob J. So You Want To Be An Interpreter: An Introduction to Sign Language Interpreting, 2nd Edition. H & H Publishers, Amarillo, Texas. 1995.

Kirk, Samuel A./Gallagher, James J. Educating Exceptional Children, 6th Edition. Houghton Mifflin Company, Boston. 1989.

Lane, Harlan; Hoffmeister, Robert; Bahan, Ben. A Journey into the Deaf World. DawnSign Press, San Diego, CA. 1996.

Levesque, Jack. "How Interpreters Deny Equal Access to Deaf Mainstream Students." DCARA (Deaf Counseling, Adocacy and Referral Agency),

Jack's Corner. San Leandro, CA. Marschark, Marc. Raising and Educating A Deaf Child: A Comprehensive Guide to the Choices, Controversies, and Decisions Faced by Parents and Educators. Oxford University Press, New York. 1997. ■

Educational Interpreting: Raising the Standards

By Maureen Moose, CT, New York

VIEWS, Vol. 16, Issue 2, February 1999,Page 10

In the interpreting profession, jobs in the educational setting have traditionally been viewed as entry level positions. They have, by and large, been filled by those just graduating from interpreter training programs or those with little experience who are looking for a "safe" place to start. Highly skilled and qualified interpreters have been a rarity in this setting for several reasons.

1) Educational interpreting has been a politically hot issue within the Deaf and interpreting communities since its inception. The philosophical debate about the appropriateness of mainstreaming, while important, has kept many skilled interpreters out of the field and deprived those children who are mainstreamed of the quality services they need and deserve. This however, is a topic for another article.

2) Educational interpreters have not been recognized as professionals by most educators and administrators. With the disparity between the educational levels of most interpreters and teachers it is no wonder that administrators have viewed interpreters as paraprofessionals. The field of interpreting was in its infancy when mainstreaming first began in the late 60's and early 70's. Degree programs in interpreting were nonexistent until the government established the three regional interpreter training programs in 1974. Over the next few years several more programs were developed but it was not until some years later that any of these programs awarded associate's or bachelor's degrees in interpreting. As a result, educational interpreters have commonly been hired as aides and paid accordingly low wages. Many interpreters have started out in education only to leave the schools for better paying jobs in the community. Although there have been some recent improvements in wages and benefits, there are still many areas of the country where interpreters cannot make a decent living in the educational setting.

3) There is a belief among interpreters and educators alike that those working with deaf children need only be able to communicate at a basic level. This belief is one of the reasons that schools continue to hire "interpreters" who have taken only one or two sign classes. This is a misconception that needs to be corrected. Studies of language acquisition in children have clearly shown that for a child to acquire language they must be actively engaged in meaningful communicative exchanges with adults who are fluent in the language. For hearing children the classroom teacher becomes a language model. Teachers use language at a level that challenges the expressive abilities of the children. In so doing they expose the children to new language patterns and vocabulary that assist them in expanding their own developing grammars. For some mainstreamed deaf children the interpreter may be the only language model that is accessible to them. If this model is in some way deficient, where does that leave the student?

Most parents of school-aged children assume that the professionals who educate their children are fluent in their child's language and have a level of expertise in their field. Shouldn't parents of mainstreamed deaf children be able to make the same assumptions of the professionals working with their children? If educational interpreters want to be viewed as professionals (and treated as such) then it is time we raise the standards which we set for ourselves. The following is a list of skills and knowledge that I believe professional educational interpreters must possess.

- Fluency in the language(s) in which they work; not merely competency.
- Knowledge of Deaf culture and involvement with the Deaf community.
- Knowledge of the interpreting process.
- An understanding of language acquisition in deaf and hearing children.
- Knowledge of child development processes.
- An understanding of the Code of Ethics and its application in the educational setting.
- A working knowledge of course content.
- An ability to explain our role in the educational setting.

This may seem to be a lot to demand of interpreters, but as professionals it should be just the beginning. Each of us, no matter what our educational background, training, or skill level, has room for growth. We should be constantly striving to expand our knowledge base and improve our skill. Educational interpreters have a profound impact on the education of the children with whom we work. Don't they deserve the best that we can give them? ∎

"I'm Only Here To Interpret"

Professional Collaboration in a Post-secondary Setting

By Danette Steelman-Bridges, M.A., IC/TC, North Carolina

VIEWS, Vol. 16, Issue 2, February 1999, Page 11

Imagine you are the interpreter in the following scenarios:

1. For two and a half months, you've been the regular interpreter in a college class and one day the professor asks you to proctor a test during the next day's classtime because his wife will be undergoing surgery. What do you do?

2. After the first major test in a freshman college course, the professor approaches you after class and queries, " I'm concerned about (deaf student's name) performance on this test. As his interpreter, can you tell me how she did in her high school classes?" How do you respond?

3. The professor in a class where you've been interpreting for the past three months calls you to ask, "For next Monday's class, could you start the videotape at the beginning of class? I will only be about 10 minutes late for class. I have a meeting." What is your response?

4. A meeting has been scheduled by a college administrator for approximately 300 prospective students and their parents. The administrator calls you and asks that you interpret for the meeting. You ask, "About how many of the prospective students are deaf?" She replies that none are deaf that she is aware of, but the purpose of providing interpreting services is to highlight the support services offered to deaf and hard-of-hearing students on campus. What do you say or do?

Over the years, it has been my experience that a common interpretation of the Code of Ethics as applied to the above situations would be: "facilitate communication/ render the message faithfully ... "—Period. Anything above and beyond that is unacceptable. Perhaps it is a natural occurrence that we have interpreted the Code of Ethics in this manner. We have fought long and hard to establish our role as professionals. We have fought long and hard to dispel the idea of "interpreter" as an equivalent to "helper/volunteer." Thus, when confronted with situations similar to the above, we tend to automatically assume our image as professionals will be diminished if we agree to expand our responsibilities. In regard to educational interpreters, I would argue the contrary.

I offer the premise that a professional educational interpreter's repertoire of skills SHOULD include the art of collaboration. I would also argue that collaboration does not diminish our image as a professional; conversely, prudent collaboration enhances that image.

At the small, private college where I have been employed for the past 15 years, I have witnessed the value of collaboration time and time again between interpreters and faculty/staff/administrators. I have seen skillful, prudent collaboration result in teamwork which positively affects everyone involved, especially the deaf and hard-of-hearing students.

Some examples of collaboration on a college campus can include: offering weekly sign language sessions for colleagues, instruction in TTY usage, leading discussion groups related to deafness, serving as an advisor to a campus organization, and yes, even agreeing to the above occasional requests for assistance (because asking for assistance works on a two-way street).

Many years ago, I attended my first interpreting workshop as a novice interpreter and distinctly remember the description given for the role of the interpreter: "As the interpreter, you are to function as a machine. Your job is to facilitate communication." As interpreters today, while we don't always verbalize our role with these specific words, we still adhere to this definition. As we continue to promote and define our role as educational interpreters, I submit that it is possible to remain well within the limits of the Code of Ethics and still be more than a "machine" and do more than "just facilitate communication." By the very nature of the role of the educational interpreter, the boundaries of the "machine box" must be flexible enough to accommodate special responsibilities which often come with the job.

Today, we still hear the "machine" definition in comments such as, "That's not my job. I'm only here to interpret." And, certainly, there are plenty of times in educational as well as community settings that the boundaries of the box must remain rigid. I would argue, however, that for educational interpreters, the boundaries must be flexible enough to remain within the parameters of the Code of Ethics and yet allow for collaboration. As we strive for professional collaboration, we must be open to the opportunities that have not been traditionally defined as "our job."

Maybe you are asking "Why do so? What is the purpose?" I would respond by saying that collaboration builds relationships between professionals, increases acceptance of deaf and hard-of-hearing students in a campus community, provides a platform for teamwork, and reduces the "stand-offish" perception of interpreters.

I am not advocating a change in the traditional interpreter's role in the classroom or a compromise of the Code of Ethics. I am advocating, however, that we, as professional interpreters in educational settings, be open to the opportunities that prudent collaboration with other professionals can provide. Effective, prudent collaboration is a mark of a true professional. ■

Providing Access: "New Roles" for Educational Interpreters

By Bernhardt E. Jones, Ed.D., CSC, Colorado

VIEWS, Vol. 16, Issue 2, February 1999, Page 15

Conflicts can, and do, occur when it is unclear as to the educational interpreter's role at any given time. This role changes during the day, especially in the lower grades. The title "educational interpreter" is too narrow. This position is a multi-faceted responsibility. The question is, "How do we define what it is that we do and when?"

A year ago Winston (VIEWS, February, 1998) did a fine job delineating educational interpreting responsibilities into three roles: *interpreting*, *tutoring* and *aiding*. Since then, Winston has discussed the notion that consulting is also a role that educational interpreters play. In discussions with her, I concur. *Consulting* may be a new area that you had not considered before. But, think about all the times that you have given your input in the school situation. How many times have you talked to parents? How many times have you explained "deafness" to others in the school? To students? To administrators? To regular education teachers? You may find that this list is long. Go to the dictionary or, better, go to the Web and search the word, "consulting" or "consultant" and see what you find. Do you fit into this definition during part of the time you are working in the school setting?

The public school educational interpreter is viewed quite often as a paraprofessional and, in fact, is categorized that way in many states. However, we can make the case that, although the interpreter does perform many of the duties of the paraprofessional, she/he also performs a duty that is quite different and requires separate and distinct knowledge and skills: interpreting itself. Are we not, then, more than an edu-cational interpreter? Might we be, to use a term that Winston has expressed, "Accessibility Specialists?" I don't want to confuse the issue with additional terms for us, but think about the variety of tasks you perform. We are not "just the interpreter." We are "more than the interpreter."

Take a look at your day (or week or month, if you would like). Make a list of all the duties you perform. Try to think of everything that happens in your job. What do you do? How long do you do it? Make the list as long and comprehensive as you can. You may be surprised to see that you do quite a bit for the school and the students (both deaf/hard of hearing and hearing).

The Windmill Model

The next step is to draw your own windmill and categorize the duties/tasks that you have listed. *Interpreting* will include anything you do in the role of an interpreter. *Tutoring* will include all the tasks you do within that context. *Aiding* is a large and varied area or responsibility. Think of all the things you do in an aiding capacity. As discussed above, *consulting* is also an important role of the educational interpreter.

Isn't this appropriate? A windmill spins in the wind and must be flexible (accommodating) in order to operate effectively and efficiently. If one of the blades is broken or damaged, the windmill will not operate properly. Are we like that?

I suggest that we are. With this model we can delineate our roles. When we are able to do that, we can better understand why dilemmas cause conflict. Conflict arises when we are not sure on which blade to categorize our dilemma. We are bet-ter able to handle conflict if we know the rules by which to address the conflict. When conflict arises, we know where it fits and, therefore, we know how to respond (how to "spin" our windmill). [I guess it depends upon who is blowing on our wind-mill.] The blades of the windmill can be viewed as contexts. When we know the contexts, we know the rules. This is where the Code of Ethics has caused us concerns. When applied to the interpreting blade (role, context) of the model, it is easy to understand the importance of the Code and to adhere to its principles. When we apply those same criteria to the other blades (roles), it becomes cloudy and appears to con-flict with the role. The problem is compounded if other professionals do not know our contexts and/or confuse our contexts (roles, blades). We then can apply the "educating others about our role(s)" principle of the Code by explaining our contexts and the roles to others on the educa-tional team. This is within our *consulting* role. The other members of the educational team do not realize these many roles. We have a profes-sional obligation to educate our fel-low professionals. By doing so, we will be viewed as professionals.

This is only the beginning. When we understand which role we are working within, we can start address-ing bigger questions in our field. These issues might involve questions of interpretability in the classroom, accessibility to content, or an inter-preted education. These questions impact our windmill and, therefore services to students who are deaf/hard of hearing. ■

The Educated Fly

By Kathy Gee, CT, Wisconsin

VIEWS, Vol. 16, Issue 2, February 1999, Page 16

Like a fly on the wall, that's what she is. Watching and listening, but if all goes well, unnoticed. Buzzing from classroom to classroom, down hallways, through the library, many people do not even know who she is, though she has been in their midst for three years. Several times a week, staff members ask if they can help her, thinking she is a visitor.

She may not have a college degree, but she has spent hours in workshops and university classes gaining knowledge. Not focused enough to be used toward graduation, the variety of information is more important than the depth. She must know thousands of words and their meanings. She has read Hemingway, Shakespeare, Homer, Austen, and Dickens. She reads the current best sellers as well as books popular with adolescents. She has taken a variety of classes in natural and social sciences. Classes dealing with fashion, marketing, and home decorating may be among her repertoire. She has taken workshops dealing with the Code of Ethics, cultural differences, stress management, interpersonal relationships, and Carpal Tunnel Syndrome. She knows the rules and calls for any number of sports. She has a background in American Sign Language and Deaf Culture. Knowledge from all these classes and hours of study now flit from classroom to classroom with her, and no one realizes how much she needs to know to do her job.

Today while I am visiting that high school, several staff members say, "Hi, Kathy, I haven't seen much of you this year. For which student are you interpreting?"

The principal smiles and asks, "How do you like your new office, Mrs. Gee?" I blanch. The principal wasn't involved when I was hired to interpret for students who are deaf or hard of hearing during the past three years. Still, even I'm surprised that he doesn't know that I am no longer working at the school.

I gather my wits and respond, "I'm sure the two new interpreters love the office. Thanks."

To each person who greets me, I explain, "Oh, I've taken this year off so I can finish my degree."

A look of confusion crosses each face, then a look of relief, "Oh, you mean your Master's Degree."

I answer, "No, my Bachelor's Degree in Education with an emphasis in Interpreting."

The baffled look is back. "What did you have before?"

I respond, "A certificate of completion from an Interpreter Training Program."

Since the two new educational interpreters who have replaced me are about eighteen and twenty years old, it is interesting to me that the staff thinks a degree is necessary to interpret. Well, maybe it is not so odd. The eighteen-year-old interpreter relates, with a smile, that staff members have stopped her in the hall asking to see her pass and her student identification. Maybe many of the staff members think they are both students. Maybe that explains why people still expect to see me.

While I was working at the high school, people wavered between thinking I was a visitor or an aide. Those in the know decided I must not be either since I had access to a personal office and I was granted a paid preparation period. By the third year, the school district was supplying the TV, VCR, and audio equipment in my office.

"Why do you need a prep?" I was asked on a regular basis.

I explained that I read the chapters in the textbooks before the students did. I previewed movies. If they were captioned, I arranged for a decoder. If they were not captioned, I learned the characters, watched for distinguishing attributes that I could use in my interpretation, and made sure I knew the story. I previewed records, audio tapes, and filmstrips. I looked for scripts for filmstrips, but often the strips were so old that the scripts were long gone. During my prep time, I studied the school play and went over signs for other extracurricular activities for which I was expected to interpret. I listened to foreign language tapes and did worksheets, because one student who was deaf took a foreign language for two years. Interpreting from one language to another is tough enough, but imagine trying to spell foreign words—that's what I did for two years—fingerspelled during the foreign language class.

It isn't so surprising that people thought I had a degree, I guess. I have been going to college for years. When I finally graduate with a Bachelor's, I will have racked up about 300 credits. While I started interpreting late in my life, none of my interests or experiences have been wasted. A person cannot interpret if that person does not understand the material being related. A wide range of knowledge is essential.

Every year the new teachers with whom I worked eyed me with suspicion. They were apprehensive about an adult in their classrooms. They worried that I would be judgmental. They worried that their students would be more interested in my interpreting than in their teaching.

Students might have watched me for the first few days, but by the second week, accustomed to my presence, they rarely looked my way. There was a meeting at the beginning of each year explaining my role to the teachers. However, most never really "got it" until the end of the first quarter, or the end of the first semester; and a few never "got it." Usually fears and apprehensions decreased as they grasped that I could interpret without being disruptive and that I could appreciate their teaching skills. They also realized that I was easy to forget during the classroom experience. When I was at my best, no one except the student with hearing loss noticed me. It was quite amazing. Some of the teachers who never "got it" were those that would look at me and say, "Tell him that..," instead of talking directly to the student. The teachers who never "got it" were more likely to show movies on the spur of the moment. "It doesn't have much dialogue," they would say. They never understood that dialogue is not the only thing I interpret. Interpreting is trying to give the essence, the meaning, of the auditory experience. I interpret bells ringing, classmates commenting, wind blowing, dogs barking, wolves howling, sticks snapping, any sounds I hear. If I don't preview the movie and I'm not familiar with the story, I can't tell always tell which character is speaking or what the sound is. For example, one movie had five adult male family members. They had very similar voices and shared many of the same opinions. They never called each other by name, and I never knew which one was speaking or to whom he was speaking. While I was trying to figure out the story line, the movie kept rolling. Because I must hear the information before I can interpret it, there is some lag time between what is heard and the output of my interpretation. However, my processing time is decreased the more familiar I am with the story and characters. It's not easy for the student to follow the story if the interpreter's processing time is so long

that a new scene has started while the interpreter is still only half-way through the first one.

"Oh, Kathy, it's good to see you," another staff member says. "I meant to look for you at the assembly on Wednesday, but I forgot. Were you there? What have you been doing?" I smile. During most of the last three years, many of the staff members weren't sure that I worked here. Now most don't seem to know that I'm gone. I guess I was a success. There go the two new interpreters buzzing through the school, hurrying to the next lesson, preparing their minds for new information. Off they go to land in the next classroom. If all goes well, in spite of their growing knowledge and their curiosity, they will be unnoticed like flies on the wall.

Since this was written, Kathy Gee has earned her degree, passed the test for her CT and hopes to pass the test for her CI in the Spring. Kathy currently works as a substitute for educational interpreters in her area and does some freelance interpreting. ■

Educational Interpreting: A Rewarding Career

By Debbie Timmers, Associate, Minnesota

VIEWS, Vol. 16, Issue 2, February 1999, Page 18

Life is a continuous journey of learning. Each day is filled with new experiences. What better environment to experience this to its fullest than in an educational setting as an educational interpreter?

Educational interpreting can be very rewarding, both professionally and personally. Every day I learn something new or gain a new perspective about something I already knew.

Since my graduation from the St. Paul Technical College in St. Paul Minnesota in 1991, I have worked as an educational interpreter. During that time I have had the opportunity to meet many interesting teachers, support staff and students.

As an educational interpreter, one is constantly exposed to a variety of subject matter and required to have an understanding of that material in order to successfully interpret it. Doing the best job possible requires time to prepare. In some cases, this preparation time may involve reading the classroom textbook, reviewing worksheets, previewing movies or utilizing additional resources such as handouts, the Internet, etc.

In many school districts, an educational interpreter's schedule does not include preparation time. Without the benefit of a preparation time, the district is prohibiting the educational interpreter from doing their best. Preparation time is also important as it provides the interpreter with some time to allow their hands and wrists to relax and thus reduce the risk of repetitive motion injuries.

One of the most rewarding aspects for me as an educational interpreter knowing that I am making a difference in young people's lives by becoming a channel of communication. The education that youths receive greatly affects their future endeavors. Knowing that I am doing a good job provides me a real sense of satisfaction, as I know that I am contributing to the accessibility of the school and thus providing the students more freedom of choice as to the classes they wish to participate in.

Educational interpreting provides a stability that freelance interpreting does not. It is nice to know that I have a regular paycheck to count on and benefits that would not be afforded me if I was solely self-employed. For a person who prefers some sense of routine, educational interpreting provides that. However, educational interpreting is not stagnant. Each day poses new challenges and unexpected changes, so one needs flexibility. In addition to classroom lectures, educational interpreting provides additional interpreting situations, including sports and other extra curricular activities such as theatre, music programs, assemblies, etc.

One of the biggest drawbacks of educational interpreting is the limited opportunity it offers for utilization, and thus, improvement, of one's voicing skills. Often the interpreter is isolated and works the entire day with the same student. If the student voices for themselves the interpreter soon begins to feel as if they have lost some of their receptive skills. Then, when the interpreter goes into a freelance setting, they may lack the confidence needed to do the job.

Despite this, there are other ways one can improve those skills and find support. In Southern Minnesota two groups, SWIC (SouthWest Interpreters Coalition) in the southwest and SIGN (Southern Interpreters' Growth Network) in the southeast, have been established to address those needs. These groups provide interpreters the opportunity to network and work on skill development together. I strongly encourage you to seek out such a group in your area and if none exists consider forming one.

I am very fortunate in my place of employment as we have ten sign language interpreters on staff, including one Deaf interpreter. This provides a support system where one can interact about various issues dealing with our profession.

Our staff serves a variety of students. Thus, during my day I interact with several different deaf/hard of hearing students. One hour I may be transliterating for a student who grew up oral and has recently learned sign language. The next hour I may be interpreting for a student who comes from a strong Deaf background. The day requires me to remain mentally alert and flexible in my style of interpretation.

For several years educational interpreters were viewed by some as "second-class." I often felt that others viewed educational interpreters as those not skilled enough to be working in the freelance arena. I think this mindset was a result of the fact that many new graduates in the field were encouraged to begin their work in the profession in the educational setting rather than the freelance setting. I am happy to see that many states are now realizing the importance of having skilled interpreters in the educational setting and thus establishing quality assurance measures. As I mentioned earlier, the education youths receive can have a strong impact on their future endeavors. Thus, skilled interpreters are required to assure equal accessibility.

Sign language interpreting offers a variety of settings one can choose to work in. If you want a job that provides you with real satisfaction of making a difference, stability, and the opportunity to interact with the same group of people on a daily basis, you may wish to think about educational interpreting. Check out various schools to see if the setting is something you would enjoy. Educational interpreting may be just for you. ∎

The Educational Interpreting Certificate Program

New Approaches to Educating the Educational Interpreter[1]

By Leilani Johnson, IC/TC, CI, Colorado, and Betsy Winston, TC, Colorado

VIEWS, Vol. 16, Issue 2, February 1999, Page 19

Most previous interpreter education, whether at the general level or aimed at specific audiences, has required that interpreters and prospective interpreters come to it—be it for a weekend workshop or a two-year full-time program. The Educational Interpreting Certificate Program (EICP) is a unique educational experience that changes the rules. This innovative project has taken the education of interpreters into the field, providing intensive academic and skill development opportunities to working educational interpreters. It is no longer necessary for these interpreters to quit their jobs and leave their homes in order to find the knowledge and training they need to provide improved services to their clients. Instead, the education comes to them.

The EICP is designed for working adults as a professional development program through departments of education. It has adopted current approaches in adult education, cutting edge technology, and the expertise of an international faculty to make interpreter education accessible to a wider audience. The curriculum takes a three-pronged approach:

• Academic content is taught through a combination of written, audio, visual, and web-based materials and makes use of telephone, videoconferencing, and Internet technologies throughout the academic year;

• Intensive skill development is provided during a three-week face-to-face meeting each summer;

• Mentoring is provided during the academic year by video, written, voice mail, and web interactions.

EICP Curriculum

The EICP curriculum is a modified version of the *Professional Development Endorsement System* (PDES). The PDES is a curriculum developed during a five-year period by the National Interpreter Education Training Project through funds provided by the Rehabilitation Services Administration (RSA), U. S. Department of Education, which was disseminated in January 1996. It was an effort to address the widespread concern about educational interpreting (Report from National Task Force on Educational Interpreting, 1991). Based on this report and other studies, specific knowledge and skills have been identified for appropriate interpreting services in the classroom. (Model Standards for the Certification of Educational Interpreters for Deaf Students and Suggested Options for Routes to Certification, 1993).

EICP has modified the PDES by adding courses in language and interpreting skill development, by expanding the mentorship and internship requirements, and by adapting the existing modules to a distance delivery format.

Educational Interpreting Competencies[2]

Beyond the modification of the PDES curriculum, the EICP has needed to develop a more comprehensive set of competencies to define the educational needs of this audience. The competencies describe in detail the areas of competency needed for success as an educational interpreter. These competencies were compiled from the PDES curriculum, the RID/CED Model Competencies, and the CIT National Education Standards; in addition, they incorporated input from a DACUM process (Designing a Curriculum, Ohio State University) which included working educational interpreters and input from regional interpreter educators. They delineate the competencies needed by educational interpreters, detailing the areas of competence and specific details included within those competencies. They cover the following areas:

1. Basic Interpreting (General Knowledge, Interpreting, Language Proficiency);

2. Educational Interpreting (Education, Development, Role and Ethics, Language Analysis, Skills);

3. Educational Tutoring;

4. Educational Aiding.

The EICP is an innovative project designed to serve educational interpreters who are currently working in schools with students. These interpreters have not had the training and education they need to successfully provide access for these students. And, leaving their settings for education would be futile—the students would still be mainstreamed in their settings, and the "interpreting" positions would be filled with less qualified people. The result: even less access than ever for students who are Deaf and Hard of Hearing. This audience is typical of the educational interpreting across the country. The EICP serves a dual population by offering an education at a distance—it serves the people working as interpreters in educational settings, and it serves the Deaf and Hard of Hearing students who are in the classrooms.

References

Educational Interpreting for Deaf Students. (1989) Report on the National Task Force on

Educational Interpreting. National Technical Institute for the Deaf. Rochester Institute for Technology, Rochester, NY.

Model Standards for the Certification of Educational Interpreters for Deaf Students. ND. Available through RID, 8630 Fenton St., Suite 324, Silver Spring, MD, 20910 (301) 608-0050.

National Interpreter Education Standards, 1995. Conference of Interpreter Trainers: www.unm.edu/~wilcox/CIT/cit.ht ml

Professional Development Endorsement System. 1995. Northwestern Connecticut Community-Technical College and University of Tennessee.

[1] This article is a condensed version of a paper published in the CIT Proceedings, 1998. The full version can be found there and/or at the EICP web site.

[2] A complete copy of these competencies is available at the EICP web site: http://frcc.cccoes.edu/~eip. ■

A Description of a Process for State Educational Interpreting Credentialing

By Marilyn Mitchell, CSC, OIC:V/S, New York
Director, Preparation of Educational Interpreters, NTID

VIEWS, Vol. 16, Issue 2, February 1999, Page 21

The New York State Board of Regents has approved a plan for the training and certification of educational interpreters in K-12 settings. The State Education Department has awarded the National Technical Institute for the Deaf (NTID) at the Rochester Institute of Technology (RIT) in Rochester, New York and the Monroe County #1 Board of Cooperative Educational Services (BOCES) of Fairport, NY, a $3.7 million grant over five years to act as the Center for the Preparation of Educational Interpreters. The concept behind this work began back in the '80s with such leaders as Joseph Avery, Dr. Ross Stuckless, Dr. Alan Hurwitz, Jacqueline Bumbalo, Tom Neveldine, Philip Cronlund, Marion Eaton, Larry Forestal, Harry Karpinski, Phyllis Bader-Borel, Stephan Haimowitz, Kathy Hoffman, and David McCloskey. The result of their work was the "NY State Guidelines for Educational Interpreting." For any successful certification process, there must be a strong group of dedicated members in and out of the field, and the above mentioned list of people was that group.

The Project Team for the grant, Marty Nelson-Nasca, Director of the Monroe County #1 BOCES, Dr. Laurie Brewer, Director of the NTID Center for Arts and Sciences, and Marilyn Mitchell, Director of the Center for the Preparation of Educational Interpreters, are pleased and proud of the work that went into writing the grant. Although many states already have state certification requirements, or are in the process of establishing these requirements, we are hopeful that the work in New York State can be helpful and insightful to readers of this article.

Writing a grant requires an incredible amount of work and will not be described in this article. Suffice it to say, the work that goes into grant writing is worth it when the outcome, in this case, means that the education of our future young deaf and hard-of-hearing students in mainstream environments will improve with the knowledge that the interpreter is qualified to do the job.

There are two important components of this grant, and should be considered when seeking any grant with this outcome in mind. Public schools cannot afford to be without the "interpreters" (regardless of their title or qualifications), so one component is to establish four Regional Training Sites in the state that will be accessible to all of the working educational interpreters. These sites will be responsible to identify all of the working interpreters, provide an assessment of their work with a prescriptive plan for improving in the areas of weakness (skill or knowledge), provide the necessary training, and then identify the competencies which will comprise the standard for eventual certification. The prescriptive plan will be determined through the Educational Interpreter Performance Assessment (skill) and a knowledge assessment. This process will be completed within five years. The interpreters will all have provisional certification because they are working and will hold that certification until the end of the time when they will need to take the permanent certification test and pass. Those who do not pass will be out of work.

The other component of the grant is the establishment of two new interpreter education pre-service programs in areas of New York State that currently are not being served. These programs must establish an associate or baccalaureate degree program and must be accessible to students desiring to become professional interpreters in the K-12 educational settings, and upon graduation, will meet provisional certification requirements. Although New York State has approximately 400 identified working interpreters, there are not enough to meet the demand, as is the case in many other states. Although the grant Center will provide technical assistance, the pre-service programs must be able to support all of the requirements of the degree, such as institute commitment, expertise in interpreting education, budget, etc.

There will need to be a lot of work put into the success of this state project, and the partnership of the two organizations, NTID and Monroe County #1 BOCES, provides the resources and strength to make sure New York State has some of the most qualified working interpreters possible. It is hoped that, learning some of the basic components of the New York State process, other states will realize that they, too, need to work to ensure that the students in their public schools are being served with more and better qualified interpreters. ∎

Educational Interpreting Mentoring: A Student's Story

By Lori Hartshorn

Lori Hartshorn graduated from the Interpreter Preparation Program at Phoenix College in December 1998. She participated in an educational interpreter mentorship program in her last semester in the IPP. The mentorship was set up through her educational instructor, Deb Pahl, CT.

VIEWS, Vol. 16, Issue 2, February 1999, Page 26

I have been mentoring with an educational interpreter in the public schools since September 8, 1998. I cannot even begin to express how much I have learned from this program. The very idea of graduating and jumping right into a job without a mentorship seems unimaginable to me now. There is much to say about the "real world" experience because, as I have learned, it is a far cry from studying about it in the classroom. This has been the most important experience and the wisest decision of my career and I would recommend every student get involved in some form of mentoring before accepting a job as an interpreter.

I began my first four and a half weeks just by observing. In this stage, I became familiar with the classes, the schedule, the teachers and their teaching styles, how the interpreter interacts with the student and teachers, the school's philosophy and the student.

It was during this time that I began to notice how an interpreter in an educational setting must take on various roles which are sometimes conflicting with what the Code of Ethics states. For example, the Code of Ethics states you must maintain confidentiality. But in an educational K-12 setting, you are part of an IEP team and there are people that you can discuss your student with. But within the team, you must only speak from the role of an interpreter.

There is also an issue about remaining professional and not developing a personal relationship with your client. This is especially true in an educational setting. But in all reality, this is a child and you cannot simply ignore that child if he/she tries to talk with you. This is one of those gray areas. You do not want to encourage a relationship and you

need to educate the child about the appropriate use of an interpreter, but at the same time you are interpreting for a human child who has feelings and needs. Slowly, over the weeks, I have thought about this issue extensively and decided that I feel it is OK to acknowledge the fact that the child is talking to you but not to encourage discussion or personal information.

During my second week, a boy became ill and started vomiting in the middle of class. There was no teacher around and the kids were making remarks "What to do?". My mentor came out of the interpreter role and into the "adult" role and went to find the nurse. My mentor explained to me that there are times when that is appropriate such as the incident above or if a fight broke out. These circumstances are perfect examples of the many roles of educational interpreters.

After the first four and a half weeks, I was ready to begin team interpreting with my mentor. Four and a half weeks of observing is a long time, and by then I had decided that educational interpreting was not so bad. It actually looked pretty easy after that length of time. HA! Was I in for it! I'm sure I did much better than I thought but I was so overwhelmed by everything that I couldn't keep my head clear. The teacher would talk and then a student would make a comment and the teacher would interrupt herself to reprimand that student. Then announcements came over the intercom system and the teacher was still talking and kids were chatting all at the same time! It was auditory overload. I wasn't sure what to sign, what to leave out. I wasn't sure if it would seem more confusing to sign certain things as they were interjected or it was wrong to

leave it out. My hands wouldn't move the right way and my mind couldn't think quickly enough. My first day was mass confusion and I realized just how difficult interpreting is for the very first time.

The one thing I did not expect was a negative reaction from the student. Granted I was nervous and unsure of myself the first week or so but I certainly did not expect any eye rolling or looks of dismay when it was my turn to interpret. The first time this happened, I wanted to walk out and cry. My feelings were actually hurt! I was surprised by my own reaction. The more I thought about it, the more I decided I wouldn't want me interpreting either. My mentor is a very skilled interpreter and now this student interpreter is fumbling her way through everything. Then it changed to, "I'll show that I can do this!" The student finally stopped rolling their eyes at me. Success!

As the weeks continued, I began to feel more comfortable when I took the interpreting chair. If I began to feel overwhelmed or tired, I was able to switch with my mentor and watch how the mentor handled the situation. That was one of the benefits of working with a mentor. A situation comes up but you are not alone, you have a safety net. By the time I entered into the last part of the mentoring program, interpreting by myself, I felt I was ready for it.

My first two days went fairly well. My first Thursday was the most difficult day of the entire week. On that day, I interpreted for almost four hours with hardly any down time. And on that day, my class had a guest speaker who talked very fast. I left that day with aching shoulders.

I have interpreted a music class dealing with sounds of notes and rhythm patterns; tutoring and bud-

47

dies where it is necessary to say he said/she said to prevent confusion; reprimanding of my student where I had no idea what was going on and the teacher was telling my student not to look at me; speech class; spelling tests where there is only one sign for several different words and they are all on the test (but in speech class you have to tell the meaning, but if I sign it, I give the answer); oral reports where you have to set it up ahead of time—will you use your voice, will you sign, should I stand behind you and voice, should I sit in front of you and voice what you are signing with one hand as you hold the paper with the other.

There have been situations that arose where I was uncertain what to do. For example, a guest speaker saying, "and they flip you off" but I did not see what the speaker did; a classmate "buddy" saying "I did do it but she can't hear me;" my student making rude comments as a remark to me but where other interpreters may voice out loud; a guest speaker giving instructions for the students to work in a workbook but then continuing to talk as they work; a teacher not giving clear directions to the class and reprimanding the deaf student. All of these situations were difficult for me and I was glad to have someone to consult immediately, sometimes as it was occurring. Sometimes I would react, do the best I knew how and then discuss what I did compared to my other options with my mentor—yet another benefit of mentoring. If I were to graduate and be hired by a school district I would be going by my own knowledge and gut instinct with no one to consult. With mentoring, I am drawing upon the knowledge of a skilled interpreter who has been in the field for several years and has learned through trial and error.

That is not to say that there won't be trial and error for me. That part is already apparent. I try things one way and if it doesn't work, I try another way and my mentor gives me the freedom to make mistakes and correct myself.

Another thing I learned was about being proactive in the classroom. There have been times when I missed something the teacher said and had to ask her to repeat the answers to questions 4.5, and 6. This was a little uncomfortable at first. But when the information is missed and the student needs that information, what other choice is there? And after a while I no longer felt uncomfortable. Another situation arose which I have already mentioned. A guest speaker asked the student to work in their book and then continued to talk as they did so. I spoke with my mentor about how to approach that one. The mentor told me to stop the speaker as s/he was giving the presentation and tactfully state that I didn't want the deaf student to miss anything and could he/she hold on just for a moment? I'm finding it's all about tact—stating things in a way as not to offend the instructor or to say that you, as the interpreter, can't keep up or are having a hard time. Another example of being proactive is if you notice a teaching style that is not effective to the learning of the deaf student, you can say something. The teacher usually reads a chapter of a book out loud during class every day. One day the instructor announced that the class would be required to write a summary of the chapter that day. My mentor promptly asked the teacher for a copy of the book and gave it to the student eliminating any misunderstandings and giving the deaf student a fair chance to write a decent summary.

There has been so much I have learned during my mentoring with the public schools. Every day has brought new and different challenges as I have faced situations both familiar and unknown. I feel I have been very fortunate to take part in the mentoring program. I know it will not be easy to enter the work force, but the knowledge and pool of resources I have gained will give me the advantage I need to face the challenges to come. ∎

An Educational Interpreting Experience in Thailand

By Audrey C. Cooper, MSW, MS, DTR, CI and CT, California

VIEWS, Vol. 16, Issue 3, March 1999, page 18

An 8-week interpreting stint at a college in Thailand gave me an opportunity to reflect on my role and activities in that setting as compared with the typical adult educational interpreting assignment in the United States. In the U.S., educational interpreters often work with one or more Deaf students in classrooms where the instructor and majority student census is hearing. These interpreters frequently work under implicit or explicit pressure to conform to an instructional model tailored to the communication mode (manner, pace, etc.) as well as the discourse and learning styles of its hearing participants. When systemic, compositional, or other variables are reconfigured, such as the professor being deaf, a higher ratio of deaf to hearing students, changes in instructional setting, philosophy, or methodology, the interpreter's role and function must also be reconfigured. Simply by virtue of being in a foreign country with its distinct national identity, minority and majority group compositions and norms, spoken and signed languages, and other elements changed the nature of the expectable interpreting role. In this article I will describe this particular interpreting setting, with special focus on situational, cultural, and other factors informing this interpreter's role and function. Except where otherwise noted, the observations herein reflect only my own experience, shared with the hope that they may at the very least contribute to the preparedness of future American interpreters working in Thailand or similar environments.

Thailand, some 9,600 miles away, is a country the approximate size of France with a national identity formed of the tripartite elements of a constitutional monarchy, Buddhist religion, and a military dominated, though progressively democratizing, state. The core structure in Thai life is the family; there are minimal alternate resources or government sponsored social supports. Those in need commonly rely on family and other mutual support networks. The only government assistance provided to the estimated 110,000 plus Deaf people in Thailand is twelve years of schooling, as well as some recent increases in support services, e.g. sign language interpreting (WDL orientation materials, National Profile, 1997, pp. 1-3). However, only an estimated 20% of school-age deaf children are enrolled in the nation's special education facilities, with many remaining at home often in situations of little resources or opportunity. The NAD Thailand was formed as recently as 1984, and although there is a small but growing number of interpreters, there is presently no professional organization for sign language interpreters, nor any interpreter training programs.

My interpreting assignment was an 8-week, June to August 1998, commitment to work with a Deaf instructor from the U.S. under the World Deaf Leadership Project's newly instituted Teaching Thai Sign Language certificate program for Deaf college students in Thailand (WDL/Thailand; for more information on the World Deaf Leadership Project see Gallaudet Today, Summer 1998, also see Charles Reilly in Gallaudet Today, Winter 1995-96). This assignment was compelling for many reasons, not the least of which being the program's stated mission and design, which suggested a unique academic environment. Some nine years earlier, at the first Deaf Way conference, one Deaf individual from Thailand, Kampol Suwanarat, described the difficulties faced by Deaf people in his country and identified a core barrier:

"These problems are hard to eliminate because deaf people are not allowed to use their sign language fully in the schools or to be taught in sign language. Adult deaf Thai signs are not used in the classrooms, and deaf adults are rarely allowed to teach." (Kampol Suwanarat, in Erting, Johnson, Smith, and Snider, 1994, p. 63).

With the implementation of WDL/Thailand, there came into being the first ever college-level program in Thailand to be not only opened to, but specifically tailored to Deaf students, using sign language as the vehicle for instruction, and preparing its graduates to be teachers with classrooms of their own. Moreover, visiting instructors for WDL/Thailand would be Deaf. However, these instructors would also be American (at least during this phase of the program), and therefore speakers of a foreign language; thus, sign and spoken language interpreters were contracted to facilitate program-related functions, and classroom instruction and interaction as needed (discussed below).

The Classroom: Structure, Participants, and Communication

Held in a large modern facility, classes met for formal instruction 3 full days per week, with additional meetings and peer-study sessions 3-4 days per week. Classroom arrangement provided for the students to sit in a semi-circle facing the instructor, with a three-person interpreting team seated to his left (when interpreters in active mode). When in a non-active mode, the interpreters sat at the back of the classroom and behind the students, in order to minimize visual distraction to the students while remaining accessible to all parties, and cognizant of classroom events and subject material.

The language of instruction, as well as the language used for routine conversation, was an important and sensitive issue not only because of the historical lack of support for Thai sign language by hearing people, but also because of the powerful influence that ASL, specifically, has had on indigenous Thai sign language. Woodward (1997) reports that although indigenous sign languages still exist, " ... vocabulary from North American Sign Language (ASL) was introduced into Thailand in the 1950's and that ASL vocabulary has influenced varieties of Modern Standard Thai Sign Language (MSTSL) used in urban areas," (p. 227). Further, given his findings on the relationship between ASL and MSTSL cognates," ... lexicostatistical procedures would classify MSTSL and ASL as closely related languages belonging to the same language family," (Woodward, p. 245). This is in stark contrast to the relationship between spoken English and Thai. So even though there might be some degree of readily achievable communication between respective speakers of the two signed languages, sign language interpreters were utilized to ensure that Thai Deaf students had access to information in their own language The size of the class was also conducive to close interaction and intimacy easily allowing for pauses in the message for questions and clarifications. Moreover, it had been established from the beginning that classroom communication would not be unduly yoked to a particular time schedule or agenda, but instead geared towards comprehension; thus a combination of simultaneous and consecutive interpretations were utilized as best addressed each situation.

Some drawbacks to the use of interpreters in this particular classroom setting will be discussed below.

Making Sense: Cross-Cultural/Linguistic Team Interpreting

The interpreting team was comprised of an ASL/English interpreter, a spoken English/spoken Thai interpreter, and a spoken Thai /Thai sign language interpreter. There were no co-interpreters for any node of the three-person team. Although this was my first time working with the team of Thai interpreters, the Thai interpreters had already been working the previous 6-weeks with the first instructor and accompanying interpreter from America. Thus, the interpreting setting and working relationships were primed for subsequent interpreters to step in. However because I had just recently arrived, there was much that was opaque.

Never was the efficacy of an interpretive theory, or alternately a process model, more clearly indicated than when I found myself in such novel circumstances trying to make sense out of multiple ambiguous variables (for process models, find in print: Betty Colonomos; also, Sandra Gish). Seleskovitch (1992) asserts that it is insufficient to simply attempt to produce corresponding language meanings in an interpretive rendering. In order to make sense, one must deliver in the target language the totality of one's mental representation of what is understood as the message (Seleskovitch, p. 3). My comprehension of source messages was anchored and enriched by collegial consultation and guidance without which the professional endeavor to make "sense" would have been an attempt in vain. Consultation with Thai peers resulted in vital cultural and situational information; their instruction and guidance particularly vis-a-vis social values, conventions, and behaviors, facilitated greater message clarity and an understanding of what was contextually expected.

Equally essential were ongoing consultations with the instructor including pre-planning and debriefing sessions following each class or any interpreted encounter. Not only was I

better able to understand the instructor's particular goals and expectations following these sessions, but also his perception of cross-cultural exchanges (which expanded my own) and how he might choose to negotiate certain exchanges differently than in an American context.

There were other aspects to the functioning of the interpreting team, and the team in relationship to the instructor, which promoted making sense. First, during his lectures, the instructor divided information into chunks, which were then rendered into the various languages for interpretation. These renderings were then allowed to take simultaneous or consecutive forms depending upon content (and usually dependent upon each interpreter's in-the-moment assessment as to whether a clear message could be achieved simultaneously). In evaluating our process the TSL interpreter, Ms. Ratanasin, suggested that interpreting consecutively promoted increased accuracy and clarity of the message as did, " ... utilizing the examples and models given by the instructor within our subsequent interpretations," (personal communication). Indeed, had the instructor used another mode of communication, namely a verbal/aural mode, we would not have been able to directly incorporate and build upon his constructions.

At times, the interpreting-team asked the instructor to rephrase, add to, or otherwise clarify a message. This happened when the Thai interpreters made the determination that they did not possess an adequate understanding of content to make an interpretation or if they felt there was no readily achievable equivalent in the target conceptual frame (i.e. not language). Notably, I often requested content clarification going in the other direction, with student comments or questions to the instructor.

At other times, the interpreting team directly supplied alternative equivalents or other feeds to one another without involving the conversants. For example, if certain routine vocabulary items were not understood during the spoken language portion of the interpretation, and were unrelated to the instructor's message content per se, synonyms were readily provided to one another to facilitate maintenance of the instructor's flow/presentation. Furthermore, as signed renderings were being given in either ASL or TSL, my TSL colleague and I observed each other for accuracy and completeness (to the extent that this was possible). Just as with any other co-interpreted situation, as the message was being transformed from the spoken into the signed equivalent, we could provide direct feeds to one another regarding deletions, appropriate stress, or other elements central to the message.

Germane to the ability to observe each other for content accuracy is the earlier described degree of relatedness between ASL and (MS)TSL. Furthermore, as we each acquired some knowledge of the other's sign language, we developed some minimal receptive competence of the other's language allowing for a degree of message transparency. Certainly, knowing message context provided a framework for discerning discrete elements.

Despite the above well-intentioned, professionally directed efforts to make sense, there was considerable disruption in student-to-teacher contact and flow simply by virtue of having several levels of interpretation wedged between each communicative utterance from teacher to student, and vice versa. Thus, any time a chunk of information was fed through the interpreting chain, the instructor or the student, if not the whole class, was waiting for what seemed to be a long time before receiving a response. The instructor reported feeling that rapport, connection and immediacy were compromised (note: student responses are not discussed here although, clearly, this and any future analysis is incomplete without them). As time progressed and the instructor increased

his TSL fluency, with explicit agreement from his students and where possible, he began to instruct using TSL (without interpretation). When this was the case, and the interpreters were thus in non-active mode, we remained nearby to be employed whenever instructor or students deemed necessary.

But in those moments that we were in "non-active mode" an interesting development began to take shape. The instructor often asked questions about TSL, Thai culture, or other related elements impacting interactions with his students. During one debriefing session he informed me that he would like to be able to expedite these kinds of questions by giving them to me beforehand to obtain answers/guidance from the Thai interpreters. At various points in the class he could then signal for the answer/data when he was ready. In this way, the interpreting team took on an auxiliary role, that of cultural intermediary, or information bearer in facilitation of classroom activities, supporting but not being central to the process of the communication exchange itself. Although at first I felt as though I had been displaced, or that I was "stepping out of role," I soon realized that I was being taught how to collaborate in a highly engaged classroom which utilized each member as needed. Nonetheless, what the above clearly points up is the vital role for Deaf interpreters in cross-cultural, cross-linguistic situations. Expediency would surely be increased in all respects, from reducing the number of links in the interpretation from three to one, to removing the need to switch modalities from sign to voice, and capitalizing on all the forms of bodily generated and referenced discourse.

Although unable to adequately discuss it here, the sign language interpreting situation in Thailand is compelling and merits considerable attention. From the very beginning, I observed in my Thai interpreting peers the same kind of professional activities I was endeavoring to

achieve: clarity of role, effective management of the target message (conceptual and cultural equivalents, etc), and working as a team member, among other things. A high level of professionalism was plainly evident despite the difficulties Thai interpreters reportedly face with regards to professional training and development.

Ms. Ratanasin's professional training is illustrative. She was chosen and mentored by the Deaf community. During her training she felt unfit for the task and wanted to quit. But she, and her Deaf mentor persevered in her preparation: "I believe I became an effective interpreter through my friend [who had instructed me to] just pay attention to the message, only interpreting what [you] surely understand. That is my attitude and my duty," (Kanitha Ratanasin, personal communication). For the most part interpreter training continues in this manner today. Throughout Thailand there are only approximately five people identified to be professional sign language interpreters, with only one holding a four-year college degree, and none with any formal training (Kanitha Ratanasin, personal communication). The status of TSL interpreters stands in direct proportion to the predominantly low social status of Deaf persons in Thailand today; it can be anticipated that as Deaf individuals achieve greater socioeconomic mobility via higher education and professional training like that offered through WDL/Thailand, recognition of TSL and TSL interpreting will also likely increase.

A Few Cultural Attributes (and implications for interpreting and related exchanges)

Aramburo (1991) reminds American interpreters working with consumers of cultural backgrounds different from their own that there are " ... certain areas where cultural subtleties do matter, knowing how to properly interpret the Deaf client's message stands to enhance the overall situation. Interacting within different cultures affords us the opportunity to learn more about people," (in J.P. Moeller, ed., p. 143). Indeed, knowledge about and engagement with the community with whom one is working makes good sense. Striving to understand where Deaf Thai people were coming from deepened my appreciation for them as individuals, as well as of a particularly Thai Deaf perspective and Thai society in general. Every exchange sparked so many interesting questions: Who is the primary agent of "cultural mediation"? Do and should interpreters automatically carry out this kind of mediation? If so, how can this be done in an explicit way, so that the actual players in the international exchange for whom it is most relevant obtain vital cultural information? Is there a culture that is being primarily promoted, Deaf or predominant hearing view, or both—when, for what reasons, how does this occur? In what ways do interpreters impact exchanges between Deaf persons from different countries?

Although unable (and unqualified) to answer these questions or to go into detail here, the need for greater examination of cross-cultural/linguistic exchanges is evident. Listed below, then, are just a few attributes of macro-Thai society which often came up in the course of the work. Some preliminary implications for interpreting and related exchanges are also noted.

Attribute 1: Hierarchically stratified society

Position in the social order is determined by a number of factors including family name and status, social network, academic and financial achievement, one's age relative to others, and so forth. These factors inform to whom and in what manner respect and deference are demonstrated, i.e. manner of greeting, polite forms of address, etc. (Jackson, p.139).

Implication

A basic understanding of relative positions in the social order is important when addressing others in order to avoid insult and impropriety. This might inform an interpreter's negotiation of conversational turn taking, or a Deaf speaker's decision to join an ongoing conversation, or even vocal tone and volume. There are also specific forms of polite address which are easily acquired and incorporated into interpreted renderings such as "Khun" (signifying respected other) and "Achan" (honorific term signifying teacher).

Attribute 2: Krenjai

"Fearful heart", the valued attitude of being considerate to others which, "... leads many people to attempt to avoid what they may perceive may bother or distress others, particularly those who have higher status or prestige," (Jackson, p.126).

Implication

Krenjai is likely operative with visitors of advanced academic or socioeconomic standing from foreign countries, for example. Several times I was approached with comments or questions that were really intended for the instructor. When I attempted to refer these individuals to him, I was met with shaking head and downcast eyes and the explanation: "No, I am too Krenjai." When someone is Krenjai, it was explained to me, they often seek out an intermediary, usually someone of higher status, who will negotiate the situation or obtain the needed information. An interpreter from America working closely with a professor could be perceived as that person. When approached in this way I would inform the instructor of the exchange so that he could respond as desired.

A second example: The TSL interpreter, Ms. Ratanasin, explained that she often feels "krenjai" when working with new interpreting colleagues from other countries; thus she will be reticent to provide cultural guidance and other information until she sees that her colleague is open-minded and willing to listen (personal communication).

Attribute 3: Phap-phot

Construction and presentation of positive images: "Thais rarely judge their actions by any abstract criterion of right and wrong ... [I]nstead they are much more concerned with how they appear to others and how they measure up to others' expectations," (Jackson, p. 41).

Implication

In this context it is important to avoid bringing embarrassment to oneself or others because it may mean that one will be judged as inappropriate. I was keenly aware that as a farang, literally "foreigner", my actions and I were conspicuous and important- right down to the clothes I wore to work. Presenting a professional image (consistent with Thai standards for dress) contributed to my own sense of belonging, as well as being considered a satisfactory representative of the Teaching Thai Sign Language program. Especially given the frequent appearance of classroom visitors and evaluators to this new program, maintaining a professional demeanor was essential.

Attribute 4: Mai Pen Rai

Loosely translated as "doesn't matter" or "it's alright"; the valued attitude of maintaining resilience and flexibility, and of avoiding direct conflict at all costs.

Implication

The meaning and use of this expression seems to be context dependent, sometimes serving as a cue to end a particular exchange (one that appears imminently conflictual, for example), or to be used as a social emollient, a way of kindly saying,"it's no big deal", and probably multiple other uses. As with idioms and other culturally embedded expressions, an accurate interpreted rendering is difficult and will probably be promoted by figuring in other situational clues.

In conclusion, the extraordinariness of Thailand notwithstanding, what I ultimately learned was not so much about the new or unusual in my present environment, but what might be possible in my accustomed environment and professional behaviors back at home. It reminded me that suspending my own perceptions in order to see things a new way is no easy task, but an incredibly enriching one. It revealed that it is possible to creatively alter the interpreter's role in educational settings-especially when it is done consciously, as a team effort, and with commitment to optimal participation by all parties—to maximize each student's experience. And that even in standard educational interpreting settings, there are many available professional behaviors and strategies to maximize student and teacher contact and relatedness. It also pointed up the immediate and vital role for Deaf interpreters around the world in any cross-linguistic forum of Deaf people. A new paradigm was made possible in Thailand: Deaf instructor, Deaf students, four different languages, different cultures, and creative variation in interpreter role and utilization.

I would like to thank Paul Dudis, Dr. Charles Reilly, Dr. James Woodward, Angela Nonaka, Surasawadee Ratanakul, and Kanitha Ratanasin for their stimulating dialogue and invaluable feedback contributing to this article.

Bibliography

Aramburo, A. (1992) Interpreting within the African-American deaf community. In J.P. Moeller (ed.) Expanding horizons: proceedings of the 12th national convention of the Registry of Interpreters for the Deaf. Silver Spring, MD: RID Publications.

Jackson, P. (1995) Dear Uncle Go: male homosexuality in Thailand. Bangkok, Thailand/San Francisco, CA: Bua Luang Books.

Ratanasin, K. Personal communication/informal interview. 1998

Reilly, C. WDL Project unpublished orientation materials. National Profile. 1997

Seleskovitch, D. (1992) Fundamentals of the interpretive theory of translation. In J.P. Moeller (ed.) Expanding horizons: proceedings of the 12th national convention of the Registry of Interpreters for the Deaf. Silver Spring, MD: RID Publications.

Suwanarat, K. (1994) Deaf Thai culture in Siam: the land of smiles. In C.J. Erting, R.C. Johnson, D.L. Smith, and B.D. Snider (eds.)The deaf way: perspectives from the international conference on deaf culture. Washington D.C.: Gallaudet University Press.

Woodward, J. (1997) Modern standard Thai sign language, influence from ASL, and its relationship to original Thai sign varieties. Sign Language Studies. Number 92, Fall 1996. Burtonsville, MD: Linstok Press. ■

An Unsanctioned Approach to Inclusion in the Elementary Setting

By Ali Blaylock, CT, IC/TC, Florida

VIEWS, Vol. 16, Issue 8, Aug./Sept. 1999, Page 9

I would like to preface this article by saying I work in an elementary school where 13 students who are Deaf or Hard of Hearing are enrolled, and that we (me and the other interpreters in our school) do have in-service presentations for teachers and staff prior to school, do all our scheduling based on skill and credentials and the needs of the students, do adhere to the Florida Code of Ethics for Educational Interpreters (a *slightly* modified version of the RID COE), do have planning periods, do have text books and teacher lesson plans, do participate in IEP meetings, do have an interpreter office with desks, file space, TV and VCR for previewing materials, and do have a mutually respectful collaborative relationship with the teachers and administration.

Having said that, I would like to share some of the things we are doing that have made a difference in the inclusion experience for the students in our school. It is additional work for the interpreters beyond actual interpreting, but it is our unanimous belief that it is worth it!

Integrating Sign Language Instruction In The Classroom

Sign language is a part of the everyday instruction in the classroom without compromising the time crunch teachers find themselves facing. This is accomplished by integrating sign language into the regular curriculum using the subject as the stimulus for the vocabulary structure and Deaf Culture information that is shared. The approach is different depending upon the grade level.

For example; in kindergarten the children are learning the alphabet and the words that start with each letter. When the letter and corresponding vocabulary are introduced, the manual letter and corresponding

signs are taught at the same time. Students respond with the spoken word and the sign at the same time. Questions like "Why doesn't apple use an 'A' handshape?" are dealt with as they arise.

In the upper grades spelling is taught using fingerspelling and signs, this results in a minimum of 20 words per week in one subject alone. The day the words are introduced the signs are introduced at the same time. Multiple meaning words are covered as well as regional signs. Facial expression and grammar are discussed during usage exercises. When synonym vocabulary is introduced, students offer the sign that means the same thing, or modify a sign such as TIRED when EXHAUSTED is the new word.

One teacher uses "Spelling Bowling" as a mid-week practice tool. One student is the caller who signs the words while students take turns as the bowler. If the signed word is signed, fingerspelled, and signed again properly, the bowler gets a try at the pins. The score is recorded for his or her team. Any disagreements are also conducted in sign. During the game students are always called on using their sign names.

Practice tests on Thursday are done in sign language (no voice). If a student scores 100%, they don't have to take the oral and signed test that is given on Friday. This is quite an incentive to learn and master signs!

Several of the teachers have noted that formerly poor spellers have improved since using sign as a teaching tool. They believe it is the combination of oral, visual and kinesthetic stimuli.

Signs for numbers and their usage are introduced during math and calendar time. Students pair up or get into small groups to practice addition or multiplication facts in sign

language. Time, weather, money and other related vocabulary are integrated into the daily calendar activities. Teachers can see who knows what because students answer many questions simultaneously in sign rather than one student at a time. Teachers have found they like that!

Teacher Techniques For A More "Deaf Friendly" Classroom

Teachers have begun the practice of saying "pencils down" while they are talking in order to even the playing field, no more working while the teachers are talking. After all, students who are Deaf must watch the interpreter and cannot "get ahead" while still listening. There has also been a marked increase in the use of overhead materials in lieu of the textbook during instructional time.

Students are required to move to a visible perimeter and call on one another using sign names. They have become accustomed to flashing lights as the signal to start a timed test or race rather than the "ready, set, go!" used in the past.

The physical education teachers use flags instead of whistles and count the exercises in sign language. Other signals have been developed for "in the field" activities to replace auditory signals. The hearing students are not only accustomed to this, but sometimes spot needed changes before the interpreters and teachers do.

Additional Student Activities

The entire student body (over 1,200 kids) sign the school song, the pledge to the flag, and that year's patriotic song each month at the Student of the Month ceremonies, as well as the pledge each morning. It really is a sight to see! Our spring Family Fun Fair performances are about 90% signed. Interpreters do a lot of additional work preparing students for these performances, but are delighted at the results as are the parents.

Each grade level has an after-school Sign Language Club, all of which are FULL with waiting lists. Several teachers are enrolled in ASL classes at the local community college and staff ASL classes are pending due to interpreter time schedules with the Clubs.

The morning in-house TV offers a sign corner (no, not the bubble). It is sign language words for the week, usually pertaining to some holiday or school related event, and is done by students, both Deaf and hearing.

Specific Modifications For The Deaf Education Program

The school recently purchased a video camera and tripod for the Deaf Education program which is used to create and dub vocabulary, spelling, and math study tapes to be used at home with family. These tapes are also available to teachers to improve their skills. It is also used to video the students signing their journal and composition material which is then viewed and written in English form by the student. It is used for other sign and Deaf Education related projects such as story telling in ASL, taping some of the "Deaf program only" events like the quarterly birthday parties, holiday party complete with Deaf Santa and Mrs. Claus (Deaf college students), annual county-wide spring picnic (all Deaf and Hard of Hearing students pre-kindergarten through grade 12), among others.

Adults who are Deaf and college students who are Deaf are regularly in the school as role models for students from both cultures. This has had a major impact on the cultural awareness. Third and fourth year high school ASL students do internships with the interpreters during the second half of the school year. This includes observation, journal, vocabulary development, interaction with students and eventually some minimal interpreting experience.

Flashing light signals have been installed for fire, tornado, and other emergencies throughout the school including portables and the court-yard. While this is a requirement, many schools have yet to make the necessary modifications to existing facilities.

Final Comments

It is obvious that sign instruction requires the expertise of the interpreter and we provide that assistance daily in addition to our interpreting. There are other things we are doing that might seem outside the interpreter's role but the end result shows up on the play ground, at lunch time, during after-school sports and at other times when adult intervention would hinder the rapport between students. Deaf and hearing students ARE communicating with each other from things as simple as "Can I borrow your blue colored pencil?" to arguing about who scored what and how it happened during a soccer match.

This is a brief overview and there are still many issues to address, but the idea is that kids should be communicating with kids and teachers should be able to say more than "sit" and "bathroom" and "stop!" to their students. At this school, they can and they do. ■

Excerpts from "Educational Interpreting in the 21st Century"

Brenda C. Seal, Ph.D., CSC, Virginia
VIEWS, Vol. 17, Issue 3, March 2000, Page 1

"Educational Interpreting in the 21st Century" was first presented at the International Convention of American Instructors of the Deaf in Los Angeles in July of 1999. The same PowerPoint presentation that reviewed the highlights of the 20th century in both hearing and deaf worlds, and projected educational interpreting over the next one hundred years, was delivered at the RID Convention in Boston in August, and at the convention of the Ohio Chapter of RID in November. A longer version was presented at the National Interpreter Symposium at California State University-Northridge in January; and, in February, a shorter version was presented at the Gallaudet University Regional Mental Health Conference in Atlanta. Several audience members have requested the presentation in print. Some of the projections into the future are presented here as "excerpts." I apologize to those who wanted the history of the 20th century (space doesn't permit), with these introductory statements:

Who would have thought in 1900 that by 2000:

- Most students who are deaf would use a sign language to communicate or to complement their spoken and written communication?

- All students who are deaf and hard of hearing would have a choice between schools for the deaf and their own local school program?

- Educational interpreters would be in high demand for students enrolled in preschool through graduate school?

And what can we expect for educational interpreters over the next hundred years, by 2100?

Deaf students demand more and better qualified interpreters

As Roz Rosen, recent Vice President of Academic Affairs at Gallaudet University, explained to a University of Virginia audience in March of 1999, "We want more than access; we want quality." Equal access to education will come to mean "equal access to educational excellence" as deaf consumers demand more and better qualified educational interpreters. The current shortage of educational interpreters will be relieved as a new pool of candidates who want to become educational interpreters emerges. These new interpreters will come from at least three sources:

1. Hearing students educated alongside deaf and hard-of-hearing students who used educational interpreters will have gained long-term exposure to a profession that, prior to the late 1900s, did not exist in public education. These students will have acquired a proficiency in communicating with and without interpreters that is also unprecedented.

2. Hearing students who studied American Sign Language as a foreign language in their elementary and secondary programs will have strong foundations in the linguistics and cultural properties of ASL. These backgrounds will lead many of them to seek more advanced study of ASL, study that leads to degree programs in interpreting.

3. The incidence of cochlear-implant candidates will continue to grow. An anticipated one in three preschoolers will be implanted by 2010. These children, if today's patterns hold true, will move comfortably between spoken language and sign language, and spoken language and cued speech. These children are likely to emerge as a new pool of educational interpreters who demonstrate unmatched versatility in oral interpreting and in cued speech and sign language transliterating.

This new pool of educational interpreters will also have earned bachelor's and master's degrees in interpreting programs that hold national accreditation. The students who are accepted into these prestigious degree programs will be well-read with high scores on their entrance exams. Once admitted, they will study diverse cultures; the language of recreation as it continues to drive America's idle time; the language of mathematics; and foreign sign languages, including Swiss-German Sign Language, British Sign Language, Japanese Sign Language, Sign Language of the Netherlands—but a few of the hundreds of sign languages that will be visible in educational settings over the next hundred years.

Research determines best practices for consumers

Anecdotal data from consumers who were educated with interpreters from preschool through graduate school will be validated with time-travel biofeedback. Adult consumers who agree to serve as research subjects will watch videotapes of their interpreters as they interpret a 3rd grade language arts lesson, an 8th grade social studies lesson, a 10th grade algebra lesson, etc. These same subjects will wear electrodes that reflect cortical areas of increased metabolic activity as they observe and recall the same lesson from their childhood. This evoked cortical data will be further analyzed to show when learning was and was not occurring. From these biofeedback journeys into the past, we can explore what the interpreter was doing that might have enhanced the student's learning. We will also be able to compare the same data to that derived from hearing students who acquired their learning directly from the teacher and determine what, if any, differences occur when students learn through an interpreter.

Research on enhancing student learning will also impact our choice of clothing. Pastels will be prescribed for interpreters working with younger students who have attention deficits. Yellow and green will prove a boost for long-term memory in classes that focus on factual information (e.g., states and their capitals, multiplication tables, geometric theorems, rules for punctuation, etc.). Interpreters will wear red and purple in classes that stimulate students' creative thinking (e.g., creative writing, drama, art classes). As students mature into adolescence, their interpreters will wear dark blues to evoke safety and security, turquoise to reduce tension. Black, the all-absorbing color, and white, the all-reflecting color, will continue to be popular in secondary and post-secondary interpreting where information is to be independently absorbed and reflected.

Technology determines best practices for interpreters

Computer-activated recorded transcriptions (CART) will offer interpreters and their students both voice-activated and sign-activated transcriptions for voice-to-sign and sign-to-voice interpreting. Teleprompters (computer screens of print that is digitally recorded from the teacher's microphone or from the deaf student's video camera) will provide print choices from which the interpreter and the consumer can choose alternate phrasings for figurative expressions, accurate spellings for novel words, and synonymous terms for low-incidence vocabulary and for words or signs with multiple mean-

ings. This high-tech, high-touch connection to print will prove to be a boost in increasing both students' and interpreters' literacy levels.

Biotechnology will improve interpreters' accuracy, too. Sensors embedded in interpreters' clothing and millimeter-thin transparent gloves will detect increased blood flow to skeletal muscles, fluid retention in limb and finger joints, and range of motion of our limbs. Team interpreters will monitor computer screens where graphed readings will reveal biomechanical data that reflects fatigue long before the interpreter is aware of fatigue. We currently monitor our fatigue by judgments of effort, perceptions of pain, and by increases in errors. The biomechanics of interpreting will open up a new line of research on the physical correlates of interpreting and fatigue. We will discover, for example, the average amount of time needed to increase blood flow to muscles. Increased blood flow means increased oxygen needed for the muscles to contract efficiently. We will know the level at which fluid begins to build in our joints; increased metabolism of oxygen yields increased waste of carbon dioxide. When more waste is produced than is absorbed into our extracellular fluid, then we have fluid retention. Increased fluid has a negative effect on range of motion. And as range of motion declines, spatial effectiveness is compromised, timing is reduced, and accuracy is diminished. These same clothing and glove sensors that alert us to declining physiological performance will also prove to be therapeutic in warming our cold hands, in adding moisture to dried skin, and in compressing joints to reduce swelling. A whole line of interpreters' sensors will appear on the market.

Video interpreting becomes critical part of distance education

Satellites that are currently used by companies to provide video interpreting will enable interpreters who specialize in a developmental or subject area to advertise on the Internet. Interpreters' samples and porfolios will go out into cyberspace and e-

commerce will prove a competitive market for schools that have difficulty in finding a particular type of interpreter. Imagine, for example, an interpreter who specializes in *Beowulf*, in the *Rhyme of the Ancient Mariner*, and in Shakespeare will advertise her skills and knowledge to a national (and international) market. As a consequence of satellite projection, this same interpreter will easily work for four school systems across four states, all in the same day. She may be physically located in Northridge, California, but interpret first period English in Wasilla, Alaska; second period English in Pontiac, Michigan; third period English in Fairborn, Ohio; and fourth period English in Boston, Massachusetts. She will earn a contractual wage for her five hours of interpreting that makes educational interpreters' salaries three to four times higher than freelance interpreters' salaries, driving up the market value and increasing the specialization within interpreting training programs. Imagine the value placed on an interpreter who specializes in world history, in calculus, in preschool education, in U.S. government.

Sign language interpreters will be sought by neurolinguists for their language learning potential

Research in creolization, language change, and language acquisition has traditionally leaned toward developmental constraints within individual — the "Critical Language Learning Years" theory. Data from gestural modalities as that provided by sign language interpreters will yield new insights on the mental bases of new language learning. This research will be held at a premium among all educators because the percentage of students who are from homes where English is NOT the primary language will have reached 51% of the population by 2025.

Neuroanatomical research will reveal that sign language interpreters have increased left temporal tissue; increased commissural fibers crossing the left and right hemispheres, increased neurotransmitters in the Purkinje cells of the cerebellum, and chromosomal evidence of genetic advantages for language learning. "Interpreter cloning" will emerge as the most divisive ethical issue among interpreters, even more divisive than the oral-manual controversy that predominated much of the 20th century's attention.

Schools for the Deaf will become premiere learning centers for interpreters

The population of deaf and hard-of-hearing students who enroll in schools for the deaf will slow in its decline, but the profile of those students will change dramatically. Where deaf schools once enrolled a large number of students with multiple handicaps, their future enrollments will be comprised of students who are projected as future leaders of the Deaf. State schools will become "governor's schools," "magnet schools," "model schools" for middle-school and secondary students. Students will enroll for a "semester-in-residence" where they will meet other students from within their state and from different states. There they will learn about the history of the Deaf in North America, the social and political culture of the Deaf, the linguistics of ASL, sign languages of European countries, etc. Residential schools will become "in-residence" centers for teaching deaf students about deafness. They will also become "in-residence" centers where interpreters enroll to advance their interpreting. Summer programs, special conferences, and weekend workshops will be conducted by hearing and deaf educators for hearing, hard-of-hearing, and deaf interpreters. Local school systems will contract with these "in-residence" schools to offer intensive courses on the specialized vocabulary of physical education, of geography, of English grammar, of Spanish, etc. Interpreters will renew their licenses by enrolling in these required continuing education courses. And the prestige associated with a semester-in-residence at the Florida School or the Arizona School or the Virginia School will add an entirely new meaning to "school for the deaf."

So, what does the 21st century hold for educational interpreting? *If we can think it, it can happen.* ■

Georgia School System Takes Lead

By Amy Elton, CT
VIEWS, Vol. 17, Issue 3, March 2000, Page 14

Sixty percent of the interpreting profession is made up of educational interpreters, according to RID. That's more than all the other interpreting disciplines combined. But as we all know, educational interpreting has historically been viewed as the foster child of the interpreting profession with school systems frequently serving as training grounds for freelancers — the "real" interpreters. Now, however, with some states embracing licensure programs, and more and more educational interpreters earning national credentials, educational interpreting is getting more and more attention. Although we have a way to go in securing our place at the "grown-up table," some of us are well on our way. I want to share with you how some committed, driven people took a weak interpreting services program, and turned it into a model for other school systems to follow.

My school system, the Bibb County Public School System in Macon, Georgia, currently boasts a cohesive interpreting services program. Some of the improvements we have made include: implementing a consistent screening tool/skills assessment for current and potential employees; establishing a comprehensive interpreting library; implementing a clearly defined chain of command, and creating a professional development plan for our interpreters with financial support from our department. Our most recent accomplishment is that we are the first and only school system in the state of Georgia to have a lead interpreter position that reports directly to our special education director and advises on placement and interpreting needs for the school system. Perhaps most importantly, though, is that the perception of the interpreter

in Bibb County as an "aide who can sign" is fading away. We are becoming more recognized as trained professionals, key to the successful education of deaf students.

Lest some take this as a self-aggrandizing pat on the back, let me give you a bit of history. Ours was a long, bumpy road. Perhaps through our lessons you can avoid some of the hardships we have endured.

Bibb County is considered a "second tier" school system, located in the center of the state of Georgia, about an hour and a half south of Atlanta. Atlanta is the state's major metropolitan area and is home to 50 percent of Georgia's population, which is about 7,500,000 (Incidentally, geographically, Georgia is the largest state east of the Mississippi River). The next bulk of the population is divided among 4 larger counties throughout the state (including Bibb) — each with populations of between 150,000 to 226,000.[1] The remaining bulk is considered rural or "underserved." Our system serves students from 7 surrounding counties — a few who are bused in from counties as far as 50 miles away. We currently employ 5 interpreters at the elementary, middle and high school levels.

As have most school systems across the country at one time or another, our school system needed improvement in providing its mainstreamed deaf students a proper education due to a lack of qualified interpreters. Our program was fragmented, and there were philosophical differences between the teaching staff and the interpreting staff. Further, we had interpreters with state credentials working to help improve services for our students and meeting with resistance from uncredentialed interpreters. Meanwhile, Bibb County's deaf students were suffer-

ing. The bottom line reason was that there were no clear guidelines for what constituted a qualified interpreter. Nor were there any credential requirements at the local or state levels. Besides, what credentialed person would want to work in a school system making $7/hour when they could freelance and make $20-$50/hour, and not have the stress of working with children? We had a long way to go.

Over the years, interpreters, Deaf citizens and advocates fought to bring about change in the credentialing requirements in Georgia. It was a very turbulent time all the way around. Ultimately, this group decided to take legal action, which resulted in a civil rights case being brought against the state of Georgia. The group charged that deaf children's civil rights were being violated because they were being denied equal access to an adequate education through the use of unqualified interpreting services.

The Office of Civil Rights conducted an investigation, focusing on Bibb County, that included bringing experts down to assess Bibb interpreters and assess the program. It was determined that Bibb County's program needed improvement and that some changes needed to be made. Ultimately, Bibb County entered into a resolution agreement with the Office of Civil Rights. Some of the stipulations included providing professional development funding for current employees to attain necessary skills and credentials, increasing recruitment for interpreting positions, and for ongoing evaluation on training for our interpreters. This all happened in the early 1990s. Bibb County was on its way.

I was hired in 1994 on the heels of this case and placed in a good school in a class with one deaf student. But I was totally isolated and soon realized that I was unqualified for what I was hired to do. Even though I had been signing and interpreting my whole life, I lacked the credentials and the professional interpreting background of a qualified educational interpreter. I immediately set out to remedy this situation and embarked on a self-imposed professional development plan. I took it baby-step by baby-step, first earning my state credentials, then my national certification. It was during this journey that I realized we needed greater continuity. Even with a new improved salary and the resolution agreement, we still had quite a disparity in the language and skill level of our interpreting staff.

At that point, only one of us had any credentials. But we had some good, strong people working in the school system who wanted to do right. So, first, we set up a situation whereby the director of education and training at GRID would travel once a month to our school and give mini-workshops. These sometimes simply served as opportunities for us to get together and talk — to be a part of a team. This was a great start. But we also needed a sanctioned position that would give us the freedom to do what we knew needed to be done to get our staff up to par.

Over the next year, I did a lot of research on other school systems, interpreting positions and management positions from across the country and wrote a proposal. I submitted my proposal to our special education director and to our system superintendent. As a result, the position of Bibb County Lead Interpreter was created. I now hold that position.

We have not quite reached our full potential, yet — not all of our interpreters hold credentials — but we are on our way. In one academic year of training and work, three of our people earned state-level credentials. That's pretty good. Further, we created a professional development plan that includes monthly interpreter meetings after school. We also have monthly workshops where we learn different strategies to improve our

interpreting and transliterating services. Our department also provides funding for us to attend major conferences and workshops. Not only has this served to help us earn credentials, it has been a terrific morale booster. Now everyone *wants* to be his/her best.

It's also important to note that a key motivator to our success lately has been a proposed set of standards and credential requirements that the state Board of Education has presented for review to the Professional Standards Commission. These proposed rules would require that anyone working as an educational interpreter in Georgia hold a minimum of a Georgia Quality Assurance in both interpreting and transliterating by 2003-2004.[2] That's *anyone*, including teachers and aides if they provide interpreting services. Our people want to get qualified before this mandate comes down.

Our most recent goal has been to establish a more equitable salary scale. There currently is not one in Georgia for interpreters. Our proposal sets a scale that compensates equitably for various combinations of academic and interpreting credentials with the minimum standard being that proposed by the Georgia DOE. Perhaps by this printing, our proposal will have been approved. Our fingers are crossed.

Finally, the underlying philosophy in our program has continued to be that the quality of our interpreting services can determine the academic fate of a child. That's a pretty heavy responsibility, but it helps us to keep things in perspective if we sometimes need a reality check. I think that the crucial element in our success has been that each of us has taken responsibility to improve ourselves and our skills. We each have looked inward to find what we can do to improve the program. And we support each other tremendously. That's real teamwork. That's our model interpreting program.

[1] *From the Georgia Office of Planning and Budget, 1997 County population records.*

[2] *The Georgia Department of Human Resources, through the Georgia Registry of Interpreters for the Deaf, currently offers a Quality Assurance standard in either interpreting (QA-I) or transliterating (QA-T) at two levels — QA and QA-Advanced. This quality assurance standard has been accepted for some time by interpreting agencies and other larger, metropolitan school systems as a minimum standard of quality for interpreters and transliterators working in Georgia. Further, the Georgia QA is the minimum standard for qualified interpreter accepted under the Georgia "interpreter law" (Title 24 Chapter 9 Section 108 of the Official Code of Georgia Annotated) working for a state agency.* ■

Team Structure for a Deaf-Blind Student

By Betsy J. Dunn, CSC, California

VIEWS, Vol. 17, Issue 3, March 2000, Page 16

The successful educational experience of a student who is deaf-blind is always the result of a team effort. It would be impossible for any parent, teacher, support staff or administrator to singlehandedly ensure the educational/social success of a student requiring extensive support. The complex and multi-layered educational and social needs, preferences and styles of a deaf-blind student mandate a sophisticated network of support that can only be provided by a team of professional individuals who listen carefully and respond appropriately to the deaf-blind student.

The individual needs of a deaf-blind student are as varied as each student, and yet, the structure of the support team needed by this widely varying group is very similar. A successful support team for a deaf-blind student includes the following individuals:

Student
Parent
Administrator/Case Manager
Primary Support Teacher
Interpreters
Vision Teacher
Mobility Instructor

Team success requires that each team member have a clear understanding of their own role, the role of other team members, and how each member interacts and supports the other. Team members must actively share information and seek assistance from others. Equally important, they must be willing and able to put the needs of the student ahead of any personal issues or agendas. On-going team success requires constant communication, respect and competency in each and every role.

Role Definitions

The first and most important member of the team is the **student**. The student's individual needs, preferences, and styles as they relate to communication and education must be addressed and accommodated by the support team's efforts. Individual profiles of interest, potential and skills provide necessary direction for the student's educational goals. As the student matures and is able to participate in his or her own IEP with increasing awareness and responsibility, the success of the support team will be reflected in the educational ownership and self-awareness of the student.

The **parent** is the driving force of his/her child's educational experience. Without strong advocacy from the parent, it is too easy for a deaf-blind student to be under-served or not served at all. The parent provides essential input and direction in the IEP. Some educators might prefer the parent simply rubber stamp decisions made by school personnel. This, however, is not the most effective relationship for student success. The parent is able to bring a wealth of background information to school personnel — and through this information, the school staff can better understand and guide the student to academic/social success. Even when a full ensemble of professionals has been brought together to provide educational support, the parent still continues to be a vital team member. The need for parent input and direction is never-ending.

The **administrator or case manager** acts as the school site coordinator for the services and personnel providing support to the deaf-blind student. From the student's perspective, the administrator/case manager may seem like a "silent partner" on the team. Although the case manager may not be the most visible team member, experience has proven that the case manager's support, guidance and administrative skills interfacing with the school district is a vital element necessary for the team's success. A good administrator can listen and learn about the issues of deaf-blindness and effectively oversee and coordinate these services.

The support team "teacher" may be called many different names: primary teacher, primary support teacher, teacher of the deaf, point person, or special education teacher. Whatever the name, this "teacher" is a pivotal team member who not only provides 1:1 teaching and tutoring, but also interfaces and coordinates with the general education teachers, interpreters, parents, and administration. Additionally, the primary support teacher must modify, adapt, and create materials necessary for the student to participate, understand and master the information presented in the general education and during 1:1 instruction periods. The teacher must work closely with the student and parent to ensure that the educational direction and needs of the student are represented in the IEP document.

To the general school population, the **interpreter** provides the most visible support to the deaf-blind student; it is also a complicated and often misunderstood position on the team. The school district employee title of "interpreter" is generally inadequate and does not represent the variety of duties required by this position. The interpreter's daily responsibilities are a blur of interpreter, tutor, social facilitator, and Service Support Provider (SSP) duties.

Functioning as the "interpreter," this team member facilitates and creates the information and communication bridge necessary for social opportunities and educational experiences to occur. Deaf-blind interpreting requires specific knowledge and skills beyond those necessary for sign language interpreting. The interpreter literally brings the world to the student and the interpreter's ability to clearly and accurately convey visual and auditory information — as well as social nuances — will determine the level to which the student can rise. Sensitivity, awareness, and training in deaf-blind issues and needs are required for the interpreter to successfully support the deaf-blind student. The individual needs, desires, and preferences of the student must be respected and accepted during interpreting situations.

Educational interpreters sometimes find themselves in the dual job description of interpreter/tutor. This blurring of roles can be confusing to not only to the student, but also to the interpreter and general education teacher. Clear definition and distinction are necessary for the successful blending of these roles.

While interpreting in a social setting, the interpreter for a deaf-blind student is called upon to "facilitate" social interaction with the general school population. This is an appropriate and necessary role to embrace, and yet it adds additional confusion of the interpreter's roles and responsibilities. Continued professional development and growth are vital for the development of skills necessary to discern when and how to function as a facilitator while also maintaining respect and regard for the deaf-blind student's social/emotional development and abilities.

In addition to functioning as interpreter, tutor, and social facilitator, the interpreter for a deaf-blind student also serves the student as a Service Support Provider (SSP). As an SSP, the interpreter will act as the deaf-blind student's guide, lunch partner, or companion. The student's personal needs or preferences for support will determine how and when the interpreter functions as an SSP.

Deaf-blind interpreters work under unusually close and intimate conditions with the deaf-blind student. This unusually close working relationship — as well as the intensity, which often accompanies it — is important to acknowledge and support. Too often, interpreters reach

"burn-out" because these issues have not been anticipated, addressed, or supported. For this reason, it is preferable for the deaf-blind student to receive alternating services from at least 2 interpreters throughout the day.

The **Braille and Mobility Instructors** both provide specific training and expertise for the student and other team members. Their input regarding specific skills and strategies related to deaf-blindness are beneficial to all team members.

Communication of Role Definitions

Various methods may be used to define, establish and communicate the role of each team member within the team as well as to the general educators or other persons who are part of the larger support network. The roles and responsibilities of team members may be introduced to the general education teachers through an orientation meeting, which takes place before the beginning of each school semester.

During an orientation meeting, or in a 1:1 setting, a one to two-page "fact" sheet can be utilized to provide information addressing these questions/topics:

• Who is the student? What does s/he like to do?

• Functional aspects of vision and hearing: How much can s/he see or hear?

• Types of educational materials used: does s/he read Braille or print or both?

• Communication options in the classroom: sign language through the interpreter; writing, or gestures/body language.

• Define the interpreter's role, responsibilities, and duties: Visual and auditory information is relayed and tutoring assistance is provided as necessary. Classroom behavior management is the responsibility of the teacher.

• Identify special space/environmental considerations: What seating

arrangement is appropriate? Use of the overhead projector and movies.

• Describe how the student will complete class assignments: describe the 1:1 study support s/he receives.

• Indicate who and how the student will be graded.

• Provide a list of the names and phone numbers of all team members.

Role-playing may also be successfully employed during a teacher orientation as a means to demonstrate and clarify the role of the interpreter/tutor in the classroom setting.

Due to the fact that team members will naturally change over the years, and substitute teachers and interpreters will also require orientation information, a basic interpreting/teaching guide of practical information which addresses deaf-blind interpreting in general, and the individual student's needs specifically, should be disseminated to facilitate the smooth transition of new or substitute team members.

Topics addressed in the interpreter/instructor guidelines for a deaf-blind student may include:

Interpreter dress: Clothing which contrasts the skin tone of the instructor/interpreter. If a particular color is preferred, this should be clearly stated.

Getting started: What to do when first meeting with the deaf-blind student

Sign Language: Preferences of the student.

Lighting: Optimal conditions and alternatives.

Interpreting: Guidelines, techniques, and strategies for deaf-blind interpreting; defining the expanded deaf-blind interpreter's role as an "SSP" for the student; as well as identifying the language and communication preferences of the student.

Mobility: Strategies, techniques, and student preferences.

Social Etiquette: Student preferences/needs; general deaf-blind courtesies.

Technical support and assistance available through various national organizations, and schools serve as invaluable resources to the professional development and role definition of the student's support team. Team members should be encouraged and challenged to define, communicate, and nurture their professional skills so that they may better provide the support structure needed for student's success.

Some parents may dream of finding an "Anne Sullivan" for their deaf-blind child; a person who might magically bring the "world" to their child. However, the strength and knowledge of a team provides a more powerful and dynamic educational experience than any single parent or teacher could ever dream of giving an individual who is deaf-blind. ■

Highlighting Education and Resources (H.E.A.R.)

By Lynne Eighinger, MBA, CI and CT, H.E.A.R. Project Coordinator, Illinois

VIEWS, Vol. 17, Issue 3, March 2000, Page 18

In the evolution of our profession, interpreting in education has long been considered the place where interpreters get their start. It has traditionally been regarded as a position with the least status among interpreters and among their colleagues in the educational system. Quite often, a lack of status is a symptom of a lack of information and awareness on the part of the consumers of our services. That, very fortunately, is changing in many states.

Illinois is among the states leading in the crusade to make information about educational options and services readily available. Through a grant funded by the Illinois State Board of Education to the Illinois School for the Deaf, H.E.A.R. is being piloted to develop and provide training to schools around the state on the educational tools and topics related to providing services to children who are deaf and hard of hearing. Among of the topics are "Best Practices in Inclusion," "Impact of Deafness" and "The Role of the Interpreter." The "Interpreter" module is one of a total of 20 module topics that is now being developed. This module, along with the two previously mentioned, is scheduled to be piloted first in late spring.

District administrators, teachers, parents, support staff, interpreters and students will be receiving comprehensive and consistent training regarding interpreters and their unique role in the classroom. This, we strongly believe, will bring an awareness of our craft, the nature of the task, the skills required to become an interpreter and, more importantly perhaps, the skills required of an interpreter to work as a member of and full partner on the educational team.

Part of the training will consist of a discussion of the varieties of certifications available. To a lay person, our profession's certifications can seem like alphabet soup with the plethora of acronyms for national and state certifications such as CI, CT, CSC,CDI, IC/TC, RID, NAD, I-V, A, B, C, QA, QAST, ISAS, I/II, etc. There will be clarification of the role of the interpreter — what it is and what it is not. One useful tool to assist districts in understanding the differences between various positions will be the "Continuum of Expectations," which will delineate the differences in the roles of a 1-to-1 aide, aide/tutor, interpreter for one student, Interpreter for many students, contracted interpreter for a special meeting and contracted interpreter as a sub. There is frequently much confusion regarding the sub-contracted interpreter's seeming unwillingness to take on responsibilities that are outside the typical realm of interpreting.

There will be guidance on when NOT to use the interpreter on staff and on how to use a contracted interpreter instead. As well, guidance will be provided related to the need for the interpreter to be involved in the IEP meetings as a member of the educational team, not as the interpreter for the meeting. Information on the materials and time needed for preparation will also be highlighted. The participants will leave clearly understanding that, to be effective, the interpreter needs to be able to prepare just as they do.

Students will also participate in the training so that they, too, can understand the differences, goals and challenges of interpreters at various grade levels. Students will be provided with activities to prepare them to utilize interpreters as they progress through their academic careers and beyond.

These are just a few of the topics to be covered in this very necessary training. The module will be reviewed by the Illinois Deaf and Hard of Hearing Commission's Interpreter Task Force, composed of interpreters, educators, and consumers from around the state. It will offer input and suggestions to bring the module to its final stages.

Upon completion of the development of this and the other 16 modules, training will be scheduled on a statewide basis targeting geographically underserved districts with limited resources. Technical assistance is also a crucial component of the program. Subsequent to the training, a consultant will be available to the districts to provide specific technical assistance to the district's personnel or parents on any issues related to the service provision to a particular child. A long-term goal of the project is to have all of the training available online in a text-based format for districts around the state to access at any time.

These are exciting times for interpreters in all disciplines. We are taking the necessary steps to becoming true professionals by implementing standards for certification, licensure and continuing education as well as educating the community and consumers of our services. We in Illinois are taking one giant step to ensure that schools understand the role of the interpreter in the classroom. This, in turn, will make it easier for interpreters to advocate for themselves and will assist in upgrading the status of those in this very crucial line of work.

If you would like information on this project, please contact the H.E.A.R. staff at (217) 479-4393 or via e-mail at dhsd0256@dhs.state.il.us. You can also check our web site for future updates on the project at: http://morgan.k12.il.us/isd/grant.htm. ■

Working With Substitute Teachers

By Doug Bowen-Bailey, CI and CT, Minnesota

VIEWS, Vol. 17, Issue 4, April 2000, Page 13

In discussion of educational interpreting, working with substitute teachers rarely is brought up. Yet, when I talk about it at workshops, I am always greeted with exclamations of dismay. Somehow, the presence of a substitute heightens all the difficulties we encounter in the classroom. Thus, I have found it to be an effective tool to use this guide to attempt to avoid problems. I provide this to the classroom teachers to be placed in their substitute folders. When a substitute teacher is there, I ask them if they have had a chance to look through the guide and if they have any questions. Generally, it begins a conversation that helps establish our respective roles within the classroom team.

As a side benefit, each time a classroom teacher looks through their substitute folder, they also see these points. I find that sometimes teachers are better able to absorb the information in this indirect way. It can also be used during formal inservice training with teachers and other school staff.

I want to acknowledge my colleagues, Cathi Bouton and Joe Loga, who collaborated in the initial development of this guide. I share it in the hopes that it will be useful to educational interpreters all over. Whenever I have shared it in workshops, it has always been well received and I decided that it was worth submitting to *VIEWS*. Use it however you wish and good luck in surviving those days with substitutes. ∎

Working with Sign Language Interpreters
A Guide for Substitute Teachers

1. Conduct class as you normally would without an interpreter present. The interpreter's role is that of communication facilitator, not that of aide to either teacher or students. Classroom management and instruction are the responsibility of the substitute teacher.

2. The interpreter will transmit your remarks to the Deaf or hard of hearing (HH) student(s) and vice versa. The interpreter will not edit nor delete any comments made by you or any student in class. To the extent that is humanly possible, the interpreter will interpret everything that is communicated in the classroom, whether by teacher, hearing students, or the Deaf/HH student(s).

3. Speak at your normal pace. If the interpreter needs you to slow down, pause more frequently, or clarify something, she or he will ask you to do so.

4. Speak directly to the Deaf/HH student(s). Use phrases like "Do you want..." or "Open your book..." rather than "Ask him if he wants..." or "Tell her to open...." The presence of the interpreter allows you to do the asking and telling yourself.

5. When giving instructions, make sure the interpreter is ready and that you have the attention of the Deaf/HH student(s). You can call to the interpreter if necessary and ask hearing students to tap their Deaf friends to make sure everyone is ready for directions.

6. Discipline is the responsibility of the teacher. Deaf/HH student(s), just like hearing students, are expected to follow the classroom rules, but may sometimes behave inappropriately. Don't expect the interpreter to discipline students. If a problem does arise, make sure the interpreter is ready, and then provide the discipline which you deem appropriate.

7. Clear turn taking in discussion is important. It is physically impossible to interpret more than one idea at a time. Therefore, it is ideal to have only one person talking at a time.

8. During class discussions, allow time to enable Deaf/HH students to participate. The process of interpretation takes time which means your questions will reach the Deaf/HH students after they reach the hearing students. Waiting a short period of time before calling on someone will make sure all students have the same opportunity to respond to your questions.

9. Allow Deaf/HH student(s) to sit in an appropriate location in the classroom. This means one where they can see you, the interpreter, and any visual aids. Also, try to avoid blocking the line of sight between the students and the interpreter.

10. If you have other questions, ask the interpreter. Just make sure it is not while s/he is interpreting. It is best to do so before class or on break. Keeping all these points in mind, you will find that working with an interpreter and Deaf/HH students can be a fun experience. ∎

RID Standard Practice Paper

Standard Practice Papers are available in brochure format through the National Office. RID encourages use of these brochures for public distribution and advocacy.

INTERPRETING IN EDUCATIONAL SETTINGS (K-12)

Following the passage of a number of laws concerning the education of deaf children, educational interpreting has become more common in elementary and secondary schools. This is a growing profession and can be one way of making school programs and services more accessible to children who are deaf. As a member of the educational team, the interpreter should be an educated and qualified professional.

What is the role of the educational interpreter?

The fundamental role of an interpreter, regardless of specialty or place of employment, is to facilitate communication between persons who are deaf and hard of hearing and others. Educational interpreters facilitate communication between deaf students and others, including teachers, service providers, and peers within the educational environment. Many educational environments have a communication policy which should be clearly defined to the interpreter applicant. The educational team may be composed of school personnel and parents and may be more structured in some school districts than others. The educational interpreter is a member of the educational team and should be afforded every opportunity to attend meetings where educational guidelines are discussed concerning students who are provided services by that interpreter.

What responsibilities are appropriate for an educational interpreter?

Interpreting is the primary responsibility of the interpreter. The interpreter may perform this responsibility in a variety of settings, in and outside of the classroom including:

- instructional activities
- field trips
- club meetings
- assemblies
- counseling sessions
- athletic competitions

Interpreting is the educational interpreter's primary role, and must take priority over any other demands. In some schools, interpreters may also interpret for deaf parents, deaf teachers, and other deaf employees.

- Interpreters may have additional responsibilities when not interpreting.[1] In determining appropriate responsibilities, it is important to utilize specialized competencies and skills of the interpreter and assign only those responsibilities for which the interpreter is qualified.

Responsibilities that maximize the interpreter's effectiveness during non-interpreting periods of time might include:

- planning and preparing for the interpreting task
- presenting in-service training about educational interpreting
- working with teachers to develop ways of increasing interaction between deaf students and their peers
- if qualified, tutoring the student who is deaf or hard of hearing
- if qualified, teaching sign language to other school staff and to pupils who are not deaf

Responsibilities that tend to reduce the interpreter's effectiveness may include:

- copying and filing
- playground supervision
- bus attendant duty
- lunchroom duty
- monitoring study hall

The educational interpreter's responsibilities and the relative proportion of time between interpreting and non-interpreting responsibilities are likely to vary from one work setting to another and may be influenced by a number of factors which may include:

- number of students who are deaf or hard of hearing in the school or district and distribution across grade levels and school buildings
- possibility of physical injury due to stress or overuse[2]
- nature of the employment; full-time, part-time, or hourly
- interpreter's background, knowledge, skill, and competencies
- qualifications and availability of the interpreting staff

How can confusion about the interpreter's responsibilities be avoided?

The role and responsibility of the interpreter is distinct from that of the teacher and that of other professionals in the educational setting. This distinction must be kept clear. For example, for the interpreter to provide classroom instruction and discipline directly to a student would be inappropriate because that is the teacher's responsibility.

A clear and detailed job description, prepared in advance of hiring and shared with the interpreter applicant and with others who need to understand the interpreter's duties, will help avoid confusion and misunderstanding.

Who should supervise the educational interpreter?

A member of the educational administration staff who has an understanding of interpreting should supervise the interpreter. In most cases, hiring an agency outside the educational institution or using a teacher in whose class the educational interpreter works would not be appropriate. The interpreter's supervisor may have interpreting skills, which is valuable, but the supervisor should at least know what interpreting is, how the interpreter functions best as a member of the educational team, and when interpreting is or is not the most appropriate service. If the supervisor is not qualified to evaluate interpreting skills or performance, an outside consultant knowledgeable in interpreter assessment and skill development should be hired.

What qualifications should the educational interpreter have?

Interpreting is a highly specialized professional field; simply knowing sign language does not qualify a person as an interpreter. Professional sign language interpreters develop their specialization through extensive training and practice over a long period of time. In addition, skills in oral transliteration may be needed. Throughout their careers, interpreters improve their skills, knowledge, and professionalism through continued training and through participation in RID. The use of a comprehensive written professional development plan will guide the educational interpreter to meet professional goals, including that of certification.

In interpreting, as in other professions, appropriate credentials are an important indicator of competence. RID awards certification to interpreters who successfully pass national tests. The tests assess not only language knowledge and communication skills, but also knowledge and judgment on issues of ethics, culture and professionalism which form the essential foundation for quality interpreting. The assessments do not test for additional specialist skills necessary in educational settings. Many interpreters working in educational settings either already have or are working toward certification. An increasing number of states are requiring educational interpreters to have interpreting credentials.

Educational interpreting is a specialty requiring additional knowledge and skills. In the classroom, the instructional content varies significantly, and the skills and knowledge necessary to qualify an interpreter vary accordingly. In the primary grades, the interpreter needs a broad basic knowledge of the subject areas such as mathematics, social studies, and language arts, and should have an understanding of child development. At the secondary level, the interpreter needs sufficient knowledge and understanding of the content areas to be able to interpret highly technical concepts and terminology accurately and meaningfully.

How is reasonable compensation determined for the educational interpreter?

Pay levels and employee benefits for educational interpreters should be competitive with that of other professional school employees. They should be based on interpreting skills, education, experience, certification, performance, and job responsibilities. Creation of positions with appropriate pay and benefits is a key to attracting and keeping qualified professional interpreters.

How does the RID Code of Ethics apply to educational interpreters?

The RID Code of Ethics is the statement of ethical principles for all interpreters, including those who work in educational settings. Within the boundaries of the educational team, the Code of Ethics deals fairly with the major issue of confidentiality.

Where can I learn more about educational interpreting?

The National Task Force on Educational Interpreting published a report entitled "Educational Interpreting for Deaf Students" which can be obtained from Rochester Institute of Technology, National Technical Institute for the Deaf.

The Association believes that educational interpreting is one way of making school programs and services more accessible to children who are deaf. The educational interpreter should be an RID certified, highly trained and qualified professional who can function as a member of the educational team.

RID has a series of Standard Practice Papers available upon request. Footnotes frequently reference these materials.

[1] see Multiple Roles
[2] see Cumulative Motion Injury

Code of Ethics of the Registry of Interpreters for the Deaf, Inc.

Introduction

The Registry of Interpreters for the Deaf, Inc. refers to individuals who may perform one or more of the following services:

- Interpret spoken English to American Sign Language and American Sign Language to spoken English;

- Transliterate spoken English to manually coded English/pidgin signed English, manually code English/pidgin signed English to spoken English, and spoken English to paraphrased non-audible spoken English;

- Gesticulate/mime to and from spoken English.

Code of Ethics

The Registry of Interpreters for the Deaf, Inc. has set forth the following principles of ethical behavior to protect and guide interpreters and transliterators and hearing and deaf consumers. Underlying these principles is the desire to insure for all the right to communicate.

This Code of Ethics applies to all members of the Registry of Interpreters for the Deaf, Inc. and to all certified non-members.

1. Interpreters/transliterators shall keep all assignment-related information strictly confidential.

2. Interpreters/transliterators shall render the message faithfully, always conveying the content and spirit of the speaker using language most readily understood by the person(s) whom they serve.

3. Interpreters/transliterators shall not counsel, advise or interject personal opinions.

4. Interpreters/transliterators shall accept assignments using discretion with regard to skill, setting, and the consumers involved.

5. Interpreters/transliterators shall request compensation for services in a professional and judicious manner.

6. Interpreters/transliterators shall function in a manner appropriate to the situation.

7. Interpreters/transliterators shall strive to further knowledge and skills through participation in work-shops, professional meetings, interaction with professional colleagues, and reading of current literature in the field.

8. Interpreters/transliterators, by virtue of membership or certification by the RID, Inc., shall strive to maintain high professional standards in compliance with the Code of Ethics.

NOTES